The Immortal Tales

The Immortal Tales

A.D. Bhattacharya

Srikunj Sadbhavana Manch
New Delhi

Cataloging in Publication Data — DK

[Courtesy: D.K. Agencies (P) Ltd. <docinfo@dkagencies.com>]

Bhattacharya, A.D. (Arun Deva), 1942–
The immortal tales / A.D. Bhattacharya.
p. cm.
Retold from the Hindu classical works.
ISBN 8182650151

1. Tales — India. 2. Hindu Literature. I. Title.

ISBN 81-8265-015-1

First published in India in 2010

Published by:
Srikunj Sadbhavana Manch
'Srikunj', F-52, Bali Nagar
New Delhi - 110 015

Distributed by:
D.K. Printworld (P) Ltd.
Regd. office : *'Srikunj'*, F-52, Bali Nagar
Ramesh Nagar Metro Station
New Delhi – 110 015
Phones : (011) 2545 3975; 2546 6019; *Fax* : (011) 2546 5926
E-mail: indology@dkprintworld.com
Web: www.dkprintworld.com

Preface

IT IS OFTEN QUOTED that the knowledge bank in the form of scriptures has been kept beyond the reach of the common man due to the language in which the same were written. To make the same available to everybody, we see an age-old practice to present the knowledge in the form of tales — this practice our most revered saints and sages followed successfully in imparting wisdom. This technique seems to have been followed in other religions also.

Continuing the same tradition, "The Immortal Tales" is being presented in simple language and style to appeal to the general reading public who may be interested to know what is contained in the treasurehouse of the Hindu religious and spiritual literature.

Contents

Preface v
1. Forgive the Sinner 1
2. Love is Divine 4
3. Renounce All 8
4. Have Firm Faith 11
5. Be Generous 13
6. God's Grace is Boundless 15
7. God is One 18
8. Guru's Compassion is Immeasurable 23
9. God Feeds Every Life-form 26
10. Strange are the Ways of God 28
11. Hara Meets Hari in Ayodhya 31
12. Worship the Lord's Feet 35
13. Lord's Name is Stronger than Lord 38
14. Bear No Malice 40
15. The Lord Knows No Enmity 44
16. Devotion is More Important than Ritual 46
17. Faith in God Does Wonders 51
18. Universe within God 54
19. Enjoy the Lord's Lila 57
20. The Lord is the Stealer of Hearts 59
21. Devotee's Concern for Lord's Comforts 61

22.	Be Firm in Your Commitment	66
23.	Find Truth in Falsehood	69
24.	Cunningness is a Part of Warfare	71
25.	Remain Unattached to Surroundings	74
26.	Mind Often Makes Fickle Judgements	77
27.	Do Not Concentrate on Life Only	79
28.	Do Not Follow Customs Blindly	81
29.	Bhakti and Gyana Lead to the Same Goal	83
30.	True Devotees know No Caste	86
31.	Choose a Time to Even Tell a Truth	89
32.	Seeing the Lord is the Goal	92
33.	Experience Divine Bliss in Raga Vasant	94
34.	God Lives in all His Creations	97
35.	Malice Only Brings Misery	99
36.	Who Has Paid Whose Debt?	102
37.	The Human Body is a Mosque	104
38.	Work and Earn	107
39.	Devotional Music Takes You to the Lord	110
40.	Surrender Totally to God	112
41.	Divinity Sees no Sin in Man	114
42.	Pray for Liberation	117
43.	Bitter Medicine Helps	119
44.	Patronize the Worthy	121
45.	Brahman is Immortal	124
46.	Have Firm Faith in God	126
47.	Purity Needs no Advertisement	128
48.	Truth is Bitter	130

1

Forgive the Sinner

MAHABHARATA WAR was over. Duryodhana, son of Dhritarashtra, was lying on the battlefield with his thigh broken by a stroke of mace dealt by Bhima. All principal warriors of Kauravas were no more, but the son of Drona, Ashvatthama was fuming with the fire of revenge. Since Duryodhana was still alive the son of Drona wanted to please his master. In the hour of contentment in the Pandava camp, Ashvatthama entered the bedroom of the Pandavas with the intention of taking revenge by killing the Pandavas. He saw in the darkness that Pandavas were sleeping comfortably since they were relieved of the worry of everyday's battle proceedings. Ashvatthama ruthlessly beheaded the sleeping Pandavas and brought those heads to Duryodhana in the deserted Kurukshetra battleground with the expectation that his dying master would appreciate his marvellous work. Duryodhana asked Ashvatthama to give him the head of Bhima, the second Pandava. Duryodhana took the head and pressed the same with his palm. The head crushed under pressure. Duryodhana said: "The head of Bhima cannot be that soft. You have killed the five sons of Pandavas by mistake." Ashvatthama saw that Duryodhana became morosed instead of celebrating and thanking him for his "great" act. Duryodhana was sorry since nobody remained in the family who could give oblations to the ancestors for their salvation. Ashvatthama realized that a gross mistake has been committed and now he has to live and survive from the ire of Pandavas who are still alive.

The murder was detected at the Pandava camp soon. They did not take time to identify the assassin who had sneaked into the Pandava camp in the darkness of night. Worst was the condition of Draupadi who was bitterly wailing to find her five sons dead and her eyes were blinded with tears. The distress was enveloping the Pandava camp. Gandiva-wielder Arjuna was fuming in rage. Consoling Draupadi he said: "When I come back with the head of Ashvatthama, you put your foot on his head and take bath after the cremation of your sons." After this Arjuna lifted his fierce Gandiva bow and rushed to his chariot.

Within a short time Ashvatthama knew that Arjuna was rushing towards him. He ran for his life. When Ashvatthama understood that his end was approaching fast, he wanted to save himself by the missile presided over by Brahma. The *brahmastra* proceeded towards Arjuna. Seeing the deadly weapon, under the advice of Lord Shri Krishna, Arjuna also sent forth a counter-*brahmastra*. The missiles collided in the air. Arjuna knew also the art of calling back the missiles. He ordered both the missiles to capture the sinner. After this Ashvatthama came under the clutches of Arjuna. Arjuna's eyes were burning with rage. He bound

Ashvatthama with a rope as one would bind a sacrificial animal. Shri Krishna wanted to test the righteousness of Arjuna by asking him to kill the sinner. But Arjuna passed the test and brought Ashvatthama in that condition in front of the grieving Draupadi.

Draupadi saw the son of brahmana Drona in that sorry state. Her behaviour surprised all. She bowed down to the son of Guru Dronacharya who in her eyes was Guru himself. She told everybody that by killing the son of Drona no good purpose would be served. She said if he is killed the sin of killing a brahmana would come to them. By killing Ashvatthama the slain childern will not come back and also when one mother is lamenting for losing her sons what is the use of making another mother Kripi also weep?

Draupadi wanted to release Ashvatthama and she was supported by Yudhishthira. Arjuna did not know a way out. He saw that the Lord Shri Krishna was smiling. Bhima thought that the Lord was supporting him in killing the sinner. But Shri Krishna supported Draupadi and Ashvatthama got a respite from a definite death. But he was awarded such a punishment that was worse than death. He was released after the divine jewel was cut-off from his head, the jewel which made him free from the pangs of hunger and thirst, from diseases and fear from thieves and enemies.

2

Love is Divine

SATI, DAKSHA'S youngest daughter and consort of Bhava (Lord Shiva), was devoted to Lord Bhava. She had dropped her body on her own accord by dint of *yoga* (concentration of mind) in a spirit of indignation against her father (Daksha) on account of his antagonism against Lord Bhava who had done no wrong. Having thus cast off her previous body Sati was reborn through Mena (or Menaka), the spouse of Himavan (or Himalaya), the king of mountains. Ambika (Sati) sought union once more with her beloved Spouse (Lord Shiva), her only resort. As such Parvati (Ambika) in her new body made severe penance to get united with her Lord. She succeeded, and her wish was fulfilled.

After departure of Sati the supreme god Lord Shiva had gone into a state of *samadhi*. All the other gods wanted the Lord to marry again, since a son was supposed to be born to the divine couple, a son who alone would be able to defeat and kill a fierce demon king. With great difficuty, the gods succeeded in persuading and convincing Lord Rudra to marry again. The whole abode of gods got into a festive mood and all waited for accompanying the Supreme God for the marriage.

The date of marriage approached near and the abode of gods started rocking into the mode of divine bliss. Now the main problem cropped up in Kailasa since the divine bridegroom had to be dressed up for the occassion. The attendants of Lord Shiva wanted him to wear a crown on that day. It was proposed to bring a crown from Vaikuntha, where the goddess of wealth and beauty Lakshmi resides. The proposal could not be agreed to by the Kailasapati since wearing a crown on the head does not go with self-abnegating Mahadeva. As such, His matted locks were arranged in the shape of a crown and the crescent moon got added as part of the beautification. Lord Shiva was wearing the same tigerskin and his upper body was smeared with the ashes of the cremation ground. The live snakes were the ornaments which the bridegroom preferred. The eyes were flashing with rage and splendour of fire. The Lord did not want to dispense with His normal vehicle Nandi and got upon his vehicle with his normal trident and tabor. Since the attendants and devotees were to walk behind the Lord, He opted to sit facing his attendants only. When others asked him to at least sit properly, He smiled and remained in that posture only. Such was the preparation of the bridegroom for his marriage with Goddess Parvati.

Now the gods who wanted to accompany the bridegroom to the wedding, started dropping in. Among the dignitaries came Lord Brahma and Lord Vishnu also. The bridegroom was to be taken in a procession to the marriage venue in the Himalayas. When the gods saw the unusual make-up of the bridegroom, they all started to go in front of the procession. When the bridegroom found shortage of persons following him, He immediately invited the host of ghosts residing in the various cremation grounds. They all arrived and the procession started with gaiety. The whole atmosphere was filled with the sound of the celestial instruments, songs by the *gandharvas* and dances performed by *apsarases*. The whole universe watched this event with surprise and merriment.

The procession landed at the bride's residence at the scheduled hour. The hosts saw Lord Vishnu coming. The well-dressed divine Lord Vishnu was mistaken as the bridegroom and everybody present there liked the would-be husband of their dear Parvati. Lord Vishnu pointed to Goddess Lakshmi accompanying him so that the hosts could follow that their observation was not correct. One by one the gods started arriving and the reception committee could not receive the chief guest (viz. bridegroom) for long. At last the bridegroom landed at the venue followed by the ghosts. The reception party got scared to see the bridegroom and others. Most of them fled and only a few came forward trembling. They were scared to come near the blazing fire-like bridegroom. At last some people ventured to propose to the bridegroom to look the other way so that the ritual reception in the form of *arati* could be performed by the mother-in-law Menaka. The bridegroom refused to acknowledge the word "mother-in-law" and did not agree to turn the other way. As such the vehicle Nandi was turned the other way to facilitate such a ritual. Now the mother-in-law landed on the scene with the auspicious materials in a plate. When she lifted the lighted lamp she could see the brilliance of sun and moon on the face of the bridegroom. She could not tolerate the dazzle on the face of the bridegroom and got terribly scared and finally fainted. She was carried away bodily by the persons from the venue. The ceremony was on the verge of getting foiled. Meanwhile, peculiar looking ghosts wanted to know the location of the living quarters for the bridegroom's party.

Confusion prevailed for some time. Mother-in-law Menaka had to come to the venue again to accord the ceremonial reception. Somehow, she did the same and fled from the scene. Marriage rituals were conducted as necessary. The guests were served with most palatable dishes. The only person who was very satisfied was the bride Parvati, whose life's mission to unite with her only resort Lord Shiva materialized.

The marriage function ended with a happy note.

3

Renounce All

UNDER THE MONARCHY of Bhartrihari the state of Malva had prospered to an enviable height of excellence. The monarch had been extremely popular due to his piety, prowess and dexterity. Apart from all this, the monarch had deep compassion and love for spiritual consciousness. After ruling for quite a long time, he had become tired of worldly attachments and at a certain moment he did decide to get detached from the same. The kingdom, prosperity and relatives looked like a big burden to him. As such he severed himself from all commitments and walked out to live in seclusion.

Bhartrihari opted for living in a cremation ground on food obtained by begging. In one of such days Bhartrihari was engaged in boiling the rice obtained by him through begging. He was using the skull of a dead person as his boiling pan and the fire of the funeral pyre for cooking *khicari* (a dish of rice and pulses boiled together). The process was nearing completion. At that hour there landed Lord Shiva along with his consort Goddess Parvati. The level of renunciation practised by Bhartrihari had impressed the goddess and she used the words "super renouncer" and "super ascetic" for the great Bhartrihari. She had expected acceptance from her consort but Lord Shiva did not seem convinced on that issue. When the question in regard to the validity of the statement was put to Lord Shiva directly, He answered: "Is it proper to come to such a conclusion so early?" It was very clear that Lord Shiva was not in favour to issue such a certificate to Bhartrihari. When Goddess Parvati wanted to know the reason specifically, Lord Shiva replied: "Let us appear as a brahmana couple in front of Bhartrihari and you will come to know about the truth yourself."

The divine couple appeared before Bhartrihari with begging bowls in their hands. Bhartrihari saw a brahmana couple in front of him asking for alms. Bhartrihari parted with the cooked food in his possession gladly. Now mother Parvati looked at her husband visually communicating: "Look Lord! What I had said is right." She was surprised to see that Lord Shiva was still reluctant to issue such a certificate. Now the brahmana asked Bhartrihari: "Why do you give the entire lot? Keep something for yourself also. I believe you are also hungry."

With satirical smile on the face, Bhartrihari replied: "When Bhartrihari could relinquish the empire of Malva, he can do so with this much *khicari* also." The contents of the statement of Bhartrihari were explained by Lord Shiva: "The ascetic has detatched everything from himself but had kept the pride and arrogance of being Bhartrihari with him only. Unless he leaves "I Bhartrihari," how can he be called "super?" He has to shed off self-conceit to go up to that level."

The explaination was convincing to Goddess Parvati. Unless one's total possessions are detatched the renunciation is not complete. The divine couple withdrew to mount Kailasa.

4

Have Firm Faith

THE MAJESTIC all-purifying river Ganga flows in the mortal world with dignity to impart a touch of Brahma, Vishnu and Maheshvara to the persons coming in contact. Just to get emancipation from the bondage of birth and death a stream of people take bath in the river Ganga daily. The mother of the universe Parvati seeing the same told Lord Maheshvara: "See Lord! So many people are taking bath in the river Ganga. The persons mortal world have really become devout and their faith and devotion has increased so much." Lord Shiva replied: "The number is quite big, I admit, but increase in faith and devotion is doubtful!" Lord saw that his answer did not convince the questioner. As such He again said: "You want to see the same with your own eyes? All right then see. I would lie on the sand of the river as an ordinary person and you will be in the form of (an ordinary) wife of the dead person asking people: "My husband is no more. The dead body has to be carried to the cremation ground. Kindly help. But remember that the person who will touch the dead body needs to be a pure soul. If a sinner touches the body he will die instantaneously."

The drama got into shape without delay. The mother of the universe Parvati in the guise of a widow of the dead person started repeating the words as planned. A stream of people were returning after the bath in the holy Ganga. Many came forward to help the widow. But when they heard that if a person with a feeling of sin touches the dead body, he himself would die, they all left the place quietly. The mother of the universe, Parvati saw that although everybody was taking a bath in holy Ganga, the faith and devotion was missing in most of the persons. As such it is evident that people are not at all benefited by bathing in the holy Ganga.

Meanwhile, a man was returning home by that way. He had spent his night in the house of a harlot. The person was smeared with the stigma of drinking and as such was fit to be called sin personified. But the man was moved by the distress of the wailing widow and agreed to help her out. He did not seem to be bothered by the preconditions of touching the dead body. He went straight to Ganga, had a bath and came to help in his wet clothes only. He extended his long arms and tried to lift up the dead body.

On getting the holy touch of the dead body (incognito Mahadeva himself), the person was awarded with divine vision. He saw in front of him the Trishulapani three-eyed Mahadeva and the Mother of the Universe Ishani. The man was firm in his faith that a dip in the Ganga would wash away all his sins, and as such he got the rare opportunity of witnessing divinity in person. Unless the complete faith and devotion is present, bathing in Ganga is an ordinary ritual only.

5

Be Generous

THE SHULAPANI and his consort were once invited by Chakrapani to his abode. The golden Vaikuntha was extremely beautiful in the eyes of goddess Parvati and the divine couple came back thereafter to Kailasa. Parvati told Mahadeva that if their residence becomes as beautiful as that of Lakshminarayana's then happiness will dwell in the family for all time to come. Devadideva smiled when he heard the request.

The divine architect Vishvakarma was summoned and to please the goddess a golden city was built on Trikuta mountain. The city was extremely beautiful and goddess Parvati with extreme happiness told Lord Shiva that the new city was as beautiful as Vaikuntha itself. The city was named as Lanka.

Now the ceremony of first entry into a newly-built house had to be performed and as such a priest was necessary. Ravana being a brahmana having sound knowledge of rituals, was called to perform the house warming ceremony. Ravana did the same with total dedication to the satisfaction of his Master. On such special occasions the learned brahmana priest is given a fee of his liking. On this occasion Mahadeva asked Ravana: "I am pleased with the rituals performed by you. Now let me know what you want as fees?" Everybody was surprised with the demand of the priest since he had asked for the city of Lanka itself as his fees. Only Mahadeva seemed to be not at all surprised. He gave Ravana the whole city as his fees and returned to Kailasa. Goddess Parvati saw that Mahadeva still maintained His pleasant countenance enlivened by his winsome smile and loving glances. She also felt divine happiness since she is blessed with the company of the most generous Mahadeva.

6

God's Grace is Boundless

A THIEF TRIED the whole night to rob someone, but did not succeed, and the end of night the day was approaching fast. He thought that another day of hunger for the entire family was in the offing. Suddenly, he saw a Shiva temple which appeared to be quite old. As such, he entered the temple requesting Lord Shiva only to help him. It was the night of the new moon.

At night inside a Shiva temple the possibility to get something is really remote. The priest comes in the day time with all utensils for carrying out the worship and on completion takes the same along with him back. He does not leave anything in the temple obviously due to security reasons.

The devotees also visit the temple in the day time only since the temple is situated a little away from the locality.

So the thief entered the temple without much expectations. The darkness inside was quite thick and the thief did not get anything worth carrying. Suddenly he looked up. He could see the metallic gong hanging over the deity. The gong was quite a heavy one and was hooked to a chain attached to the ceiling of the temple.

The gong was made of brass and could fetch a handsome amount if sold in the market. As such, the thief wanted to take the same away. It was at quite a height and no stool, etc. was available nearby. It was beyond the reach of a human height to detatch the gong without a stool or a ladder.

The thief looked up helplessly. But it is said that necessity is the mother of invention. As such, a novel method struck the mind of the thief to go up to the gong. The *linga* emblem or idol of Lord Shiva was in front of him. The thief decided to go up the *Shivalinga* and reach the gong. As such he proceeded to use the novel method and ask for forgiveness of Lord Shiva for committing the sin after getting the gong in his possession. But he was not ready for the incident which followed. The moment he kept his foot on top of the *linga* there was a loud sound of high decibels resembling a thunder-strike. When he got terribly nervous due to the loud sound, he fell on the ground.

The thief suddenly saw a divine figure in front of him. The dark temple was now illuminated with the light emitted by the figure. The head was decorated with matted hair locks with a crescent moon, the body was smeared with the ashes of the cremation ground. In His hands there was a trident and a tabor. The figure had three eyes and ornaments of snakes on the body and was wearing skin of the tiger. The thief did not have any difficulty to recognize the figure as Lord Shiva only. When the thief was trembling due to the fear of getting punished due to the sin committed, he was surprised to hear Lord Shiva telling: "I am pleased with you and you can ask whatever you want."

Recovering from the initial shock the thief submitted: "Lord! Possibly You have not noticed that I had come to this temple for stealing the gong only. I have not come here to worship You. I have not worshipped You at all, then how come you are pleased with me. Actually I should be punished for the sin committed."

The thief was surprised that Lord Shiva smiled at his reply. Without answering the thief Lord Shiva said: "If you want to ask for something do it quickly, otherwise I will enter in the idol again."

The thief was spellbound with the nectarine beauty of His lotus-like countenance enlivened by His winsome smile and loving glances. Recovering somehow the thief said: "I only want to know from you the reason why You are pleased with me." The Lord replied: "My son! To please Me people offer flowers with sandal paste, leaf of wood-apple tree, milk, the Ganga-water, offerings as fruits, rice, etc. but you have offered yourself. Since nobody did so earlier, I am very pleased with you."

The thief was not in a position to ask for a boon. As such Mahadeva on His own granted him the Abode of Shiva and disappeared within the *Shivalinga*. The thief stood there motionless shedding tears for getting a chance vision of Lord Shiva entirely due to the grace of the Lord.

7

God is One

HOLDING FESTIVALS in all religions has got a basic purpose. It reminds everybody that the Almighty in the form of divine bliss is always present in the mortal beings. Festivals give opportunities to identify the same. Those who are able to identify the same get a chance to think of living constantly in association of the same. As such new occasions are created to remain in the state of happiness from time to time. Such an occasion is the celebration of the (sixtieth) marriage day of very old couples when all the rituals of marriage are repeated after sixty years keeping the old couple in the centre. The celebration is witnessed by a large crowd of invited persons ending with taking blessings from the old couple. The celebration is known as *shashtha-purti*-marriage.

Once a similar festival was thought of in the land of gods and goddesses also. Everybody there, wanted some special occasion when all could meet during a festival. All approached Shiva–Parvati to agree to hold such a festival keeping them in the centre as an old couple completing sixty years of married life. Sachchidananda being the treasury of happiness agreed readily to give happiness to others. The venue of the wedding ceremony was decorated by expert hands and the couple were also tastefully dressed with marriage raiments and ornaments. All assembled at the venue at the right time with ceremonial attires. Heaven started humming with the sound of the celestial instruments. Drums and kettledrums were played by experts. *Gandharvas* started singing, *Apsarases* started dancing. The whole atmosphere changed and everybody was in a happy mode. Dignitaries started arriving. Even Lord Vishnu and Lord Brahma came dressed up to take part in the celebrations.

The fire in the sacrificial pit got initiated after all preparations of the marriage ceremony were completed. The bride and the groom were brought to the venue of the wedding ceremony. Everybody assembled happily to take part in the heavenly marriage ceremony. The atmosphere was dense with incense, resin, perfumes, rose water, etc. The celestial sage Narada took charge as priest of the ceremony.

The marriage ceremony started in the midst of fun and gaiety. Narada started the oblation ceremony in the sacrificial fire. All present were enjoying the events carried out one by one in the proper sequence and both the bride and the groom were co-operating with the priest to give happiness to everybody. Now priest Narada wanted to increase the joy of everybody. He suddenly said: "During marriage ceremony the names of the forefathers are necessary. As such the groom must tell me his father's name." Mahadeva is eternal, immortal and absolute Himself but the persons who had assembled wanted to know what he would say. The groom felt uncomfortable with such a question put to him in public. He was not replying, but the priest was bent upon knowing that and announced that without the father's name the ceremony/celebration could not go on. At last Lord Shiva had to speak out to save everybody's merrymaking. He saw Lord Brahma with a white beard sitting at a distance. So he managed the situation by calling Lord Brahma His father. Narada with a loud voice chanted the entire verse with Lord Brahma as the father of the groom and offered oblation in the sacrificial fire. The situation which was going out of control got saved somehow.

But the problem for Lord Shiva was far from over. Again the priest intervened and asked that during the marriage ceremony the name of the grandfather of the groom is also mandatory and hence the same may please be told immediately. The ball was again in the court of Lord Shiva. He somehow wanted to skip this but the priest being very strict in the matter of ceremonial acts, insisted that the name of grandfather is a must for continuation of the ceremony. The funfare was on the verge of getting destroyed. This time Lord Shiva remembered that Lord Brahma was born from the lotus-like navel of Lord Vishnu and hence He said that the name of his grandfather is Lord Vishnu, seated very near to him. All enjoyed the fun and the oblation to fire was offered by naming Lord Vishnu as the grandfather of the groom. The chaotic condition in the celebration subsided making everybody happy. After all, the basic purpose of the marriage ceremony was to enjoy with the company of others.

But who knew that more problem was in the offing for the groom? Now the priest demanded the name of the great-grandfather of the groom to satisfy the rules prescribed for worshipping three steps up in the ancestry ladder. This has become a real problem for the groom since He could find nobody available. Hence, He decided to keep quiet against the demand by the priest. The decibels in the assembly soared and the celebration came on the verge of getting abandoned. When everybody looked worried the groom maintained his nectarine beauty of his lotus-like countenance enlivened by his winsome smile and loving glances. The bride was amused over the situation created by the priest. On the verge of collapse of the celebration, a solution came from the groom only. He said: "I shall definitely tell everybody the name of my great-grandfather but since the name is very pious in nature, at the time of taking the name, playing of the auspicious and propitious instruments with a high note is essential. The priest was very prompt to order the instrument players to do the same. Drums, kettledrums, trumpets, and conches started filling the whole atmosphere with sound at high note. The Groom now whispered in the ear of the priest: "Grandfather's father being myself only take my name as the great-grandfather." The oblation in the sacrificial fire with that name was given but since the universe was filled with a deafening noise, nobody could hear the same. Only the priest smiled.

Other ceremonial events were carried out giving enormous pleasures to the attending crowd. Exchange of garlands was also not left out. The marriage ceremony ended with lot of funfare and merriment. The visitors were served with delicious food. The visitors departed after showing due respect to the divine couple.

The theme behind the story is that the creation, preservation and dissolution is carried out by *Brahman* or the Supreme God, only through Lord Brahma, Lord Vishnu and Lord Shiva respectively in that sequence.

8

Guru's Compassion is Immeasurable

TARAPITHA WAS at that time reverberating with the sadhana of Goddess Tara by Her most beloved son Bama. The ascetic was spending the whole time with his holy Mother. Ascetic Bama was in a playful mood and mother Tara was continuously active satisfying the different desires of the son. Devotees were assembling at the holy place to witness the devotion of ascetic Bama. Bama was Baba to them.

That evening ascetic Bama was sitting on the platform of the holy temple along with four persons and talking about the glory of mother Tara. Suddenly the child-like ascetic made a peculiar demand to the visiting devotees. He wanted to eat fish and asked the persons present to arrange for the same. The Tarapith cremation ground was situated far off from the locality and a makeshift market facility was only available on one day in a week. It was an odd day and getting fish in that dark evening time was next to impossible. The devotees tried to pacify him but Bama remained firm in his demand.

One of them asked: "Baba! Tell me, where can I go and fetch fish at this hour?"

Bama replied: "Go that side."

The devotees saw that Baba was pointing towards the dense forest behind the main temple. The area was pitch dark and covered with bushy undergrowth. The place was not safe to visit. But the Baba had to be pleased.

One of the devotees agreed to go that way, but he was very sure that the chance of getting fish at that odd hour in that desolate place was nil. After covering a long distance, he stopped and thought that going further inside the forest would be dangerous. When he was about to turn back, he saw a dark village woman coming from the other side. The woman had a wicker basket on her head.

He was not required to ask. The question came from her side only: "Want fish?"

The devotee stood flabbergasted. He wondered at the coincidence — the pious man wanted to eat fish and this woman wanted to give fish! The devotee could say "yes" only by nodding his head. The woman took down the basket which had a big *rohu* fish. The devotee paid the price of six *paisa* and took away the fish.

When the ascetic Bama saw the fish, he asked: "Where could you get it?"

The devotee replied: "In the forest area behind the Tara temple. I bought the fish from a black woman who wanted to sell it.

The information gave the child-like Ascetic great pleasure. In the spurt of happiness he started dancing with the glory of the name of mother Tara. Suddenly, he looked at the devotee and with loud laughter, said:

"You saw the Mother. You neither recognized Her nor could catch Her."

The devotee ran back to the spot where he had seen the black woman with the fish. When he reached the spot he found nobody. The wicker basket with the six *paise* he had given as cost of the fish was lying on the ground.

If the incident is termed as supernatural how can the fish, wicker basket and six *paise* be called the same.

The devotee who met mother Tara and bought the fish understood that the great ascetic Baba wanted to give an opportunity to the devotee to see the Universal Mother with his own eyes. Baba's desire to eat fish at that odd hour was to bestow His compassion on the devotee.

9

God Feeds Every Life-form

LORD NARAYANA is known to be the protector of the whole world but doubt existed in the mind of Goddess Lakshmi since she is known to be the Goddess of beauty and prosperity and the title protector is better applicable to Her than to the Lord. Jokingly the Goddess told the Lord to prove the same after keeping an ant in a sealed container. She said : "Lord! If you are the protector of the world then arrange food for the ant which I have kept and sealed in this container." Lord Narayana simply smiled at the words spoken by his consort.

Later on She opened the lid of the container to examine the condition of the ant arrested by her inside the empty container three days back. She looked with astonishment that the ant was quite happy eating a grain of rice. So it was proved that the ant was protected by somebody, when it was denied food by the Goddess of prosperity Herself. The question haunted Her mind: "How the grain of rice was transported inside the locked container?"

She preferred to put her question directly to the Lord only. When she approached the Lord, the Lord already knew what the Goddess wanted to know from Him. But

He waited for the question. Goddess Lakshmi saw that the Lord was maintaining pleasant countenance with a winsome smile. Anyway, the question was formally put before the Lord. The Lord replied: "I had put a grain of rice on the holy mark of sandal paste on your forehead when you were about to close the lid of the container since I knew your plans earlier."

Goddess Lakshmi accepted that the statement that the Lord is the protector of the world is correct without doubt.

10

Strange are the Ways of God

THE CELESTIAL SAGE Narada one day had gone to Vaikuntha to have audience with the Lord. He was surprised to know that Narayana wanted to visit the world of mortals himself. Narada wanted to accompany the Lord. Both posed as poor brahmanas and reached the destination.

The brahmanas with begging bowls came to the door of a rich landlord. The security guards did not allow the two brahmanas to meet the landlord. When they refused to move away the brahmanas were arrested and produced before the landlord for appropriate action against them. The brahmanas when produced before the landlord, begged for alms. They were admonished with bitter words: "Young persons living on begging alms? Can't you work and earn? You should be taught a lesson for all time to come." They were given left-over food and were pushed out of the gate by the neck. Sage Narada was astonished to see that Lord Narayana was still maintaining his pleasant countenance. He got more surprised when the Lord offered benediction with loving glances to the landlord: "May you extend and grow further in prosperity." They were physically driven out of the mansion. The sage Narada was extremely angry at the behaviour of the rich landlord towards Lord Narayana, who seemed least bothered about the happenings.

The brahmanas were again on the move. After walking for some time they could see a cottage at a distance. The Lord wanted to visit the cottage. When the brahmanas begged for alms, they were called inside the cottage and offered seats after their feet were washed. The couple living in the cottage looked quite old and poor. It was apparent that the couple were about to start their frugal midday meals when the visitors called. As a mark of courtesy the old couple offered their own food (in the form of cooked rice) to the visitors. The brahmanas accepted the food and Narayana looked extremely pleased with the couple.

After taking a little rest Lord Narayana wanted to know from the old woman how they were able to run their household. The woman replied: "We have a cow. Of the milk we get daily, half the quantity we sell out which fetches us two days' one-time meal every week. The other half we consume ourselves." Hearing this statement the first thought which flashed in the mind of sage Narada was that the meal that they had just consumed will keep the old couple hungry for a full week. He looked with anxiety towards the Lord who seemed to be least bothered about the repercussions. But the parting words given by the Lord to the old couple looked most inappropriate when Narayana gave the blessing: "Let the cow die at the earliest."

The celestial sage Narada was totally dissatisfied with the blessings given by the Lord on the two occasions. They were walking back to mark the end of adventure for the day. The devotee with due submission wanted to know from the Lord the reason for awarding such peculiar blessings. Lord Narayana was smiling all the way, keeping his pleasing countenance and was not replying to the question. When the devotee Narada insisted to know the same, the Lord replied: "The landlord was seen burning with the fire of passion and arrogance and I have enlivened the same so that he gets purified after getting burnt out. And the old couple were standing at the door of Vaikuntha and the only hindrance was their love towards the cow. Hence, I have blessed them that the cow dies to allow them emancipation."

The reasonings given by the Lord made the celestial sage Narada speechless since the same was beyond the imagination of any normal person.

11

Hara Meets Hari in Ayodhya

LORD SHULAPANI had always been interested in the divine acts of Lord Chakrapani performed by him to keep his commitment of manifestation during the decline of righteousness and growth of unrighteousness. Now he had landed at the palace of King Dasharatha at Ayodhya. Mahadeva wanted to see his dear friend displaying his divine play as a baby human being. So He decided to visit him in person. When he thought of taking his consort also along with him, he remembered the confusion created last time when he had visited sage Kumvaj and the whole episode ended with loss of Sati and wreck of Daksha's sacrifice. As such, He decided to go alone this time. But crow Bhushundi insisted to accompany him in this divine visit. Lord Shiva informed his consort that he will be out for some time and without divulging his destination He left Kailasa.

Both landed at Ayodhya. The Lord wanted to keep their identity secret. As such appearing in person in the gynaeceum of King Dasharatha was out of question. On thinking deeply in the matter, it was planned to enter the place as a palmist. As such, Lord Shiva disguised as an old palmist with a long white beard on his chin. He took the name, Baba Girijanath. The divine crow

Bhushundi became the assistant of the palmist as Bhushundi Das. Both sat on the wayside under a tree and with the advertising expertise of the assistant, Baba Girijanath got established in no time and a huge number of people started coming to him for the knowledge and redress of future events. Within a very short time he obtained fame as an omniscient palmist having knowledge of past, present and future. The news of the expertise of palmist, reached the gynaeceum of King Dasharatha also and the palmist got a call from the same. Mother Kaushalya wanted to know about the future of her son. As such, the planning to enter the gynaeceum to see Chakrapani as a baby in the cradle clicked.

But the hazard was still in the offing. Entry to the inner apartments of the royal palace which is generally barred to male outsiders, had become tough due to objection from the gateman to allow entry of two persons when permission was only granted for one person, viz. the astrologer. The gateman was told that the assistant is also equally an expert, then the visitors were told that in that case only the assistant could go. The gateman was then told that the expertise of the chief fortune-teller is a must in this case. Then the gateman wanted to allow the astrologer only but the reason put forward to defend the entry of both was that the astrologer is quite aged and he requires a helping hand in this case. At last the gateman got disgusted with both the persons and in a rage allowed both to enter.

After a while the scene was quite pleasing to the eyes. Baby Chakrapani was lying on the lap of Shulapani and both were enjoying the company of each other. Baba Girijanath had forgotten the purpose for which he was allowed entry to the inner apartments. Baba got back to action when He heard mother Kaushalya telling : "Baba! I want to know about my son from you." The astrologer started telling: "This baby is rich with divine symptoms. In future He will get recognition as a superman with high grade of merit. His name only will give emancipation from the bondage of birth and death." Baba Girijanath thought that he would be spared by the ladies of the gynaeceum now. But his idea got a jolt when he heard mother Kaushalya telling: "O omniscient Baba! I want to know about the future of the baby. Kindly tell me the same."

Baba Girijanath sensed the danger but he had to tell since he had come inside as an astrologer knowing the past, present and future of the baby. Hence, he commenced: "This baby later on, will become immensely powerful. He will kill many a demon in time to come. At a tender age only an eminent sage will come to take him along with his younger brother away." Now with these words mother Kaushalya got panicky. As such the astrologer wanted to pacify the mother. He said : "Your royal palace, thereafter, would be decorated with a beautiful daughter-in-law and then however . . . ," Baba Girijanath was about to spell out future events (viz. departure to the forest, abduction of Sita, Rama-Ravana battle, etc.) but he had to stop under instruction of the divine baby on his lap giving a tug to his white long beard within the reach of the baby. Some caution was necessary since hearing those future events mother Kaushalya would have become extremely sorry. Now departure was necessary. Baba showed shortage of time and got respite from the ladies of the palace. He was paid a handsome reward for his predictions.

On return to Kailasa, He was questioned by the consort: "Lord! You went for a short period but you took so much time?" Lord Shiva knew that the Mother of the Universe Parvati has already come to know about every incident, hence He had to tell all. Now a question again: "You went alone, why? Permit me to go alone to get a glimpse of Narayana." Permission was granted happily. Goddess Parvati went inside Ayodhya's royal palace in the guise of a clay toy seller and could have the coveted glimpse of Narayana without any problem. Can anybody stop Shakti from performing as she likes?

12

Worship the Lord's feet

LORD SHRI RAMACHANDRA was proceeding towards his forest kingdom. He was accompanied by his wife Sita Devi and younger brother Lakshmana. They all were dressed as ascetics. When the Lord reached the bank of the river Ganga, he somehow convinced the minister Sumanta to go back to Ayodhya. Sumanta did not disobey the order but while parting he looked like a person having been robbed of every possession in life. Lord Ramachandra then requested the boatman to take them to the other bank of the river. Here, the fallacy is difficult to understand. The Lord who is capable of bestowing emancipation from the bondage of birth and death (viz. ocean of the world) was seeking help from a boatman to cross a river! The *lila* is extremely difficult to understand.

Ganga was horripilated to see the lotus feet of the Lord which she had seen earlier also. In the Vamana incarnation when Lord Brahma had seen the lotus feet of the Lord he had washed the same and the water was collected by him in his *kamandalu.* This water after getting the touch of Lord Shiva had flown to the earth for purifying and emancipating human beings and was named Ganga. Hence, the water of Ganga having the rare touch of Lord Brahma, Lord Vishnu and Lord

Maheshvara, has the name Brahmabari (viz. *Brahman* in liquid form). As such, the extreme pleasure of Ganga by seeing the lotus feet of the Lord again can be well understood.

But the boatman seemed to be not in a hurry to take the Lord in his boat since he knew the divine grace of the lotus feet of the Lord. He had the information that in the *ashrama* of sage Gautama by the grace of touch of the dust of the lotus feet of the Lord the rocky Ahalya had been reconverted into Ahalya with a worldly human body. The boatman informed Lord Shri Ramachandra bluntly: "I know the power of those feet. If my wooden boat turns into a golden boat then the same will sink and my only way to earn money to continue living, would be gone. As such, without washing those feet, taking You in the boat is not possible. I shall arrange for washing the feet first." Ganga was totally surprised. It is a great fortune for the boatman that Lord Himself has come to him for service and the boatman has started bargaining with the Lord! Lord had to agree to the condition imposed by the boatman. He brought the water of Ganga only to arrange the wash. With all respect, the boatman then washed the feet of the Lord and he looked to be quite satisfied with the same. Now the Lord Shri Ramachandra said: "O boatman! Do not delay now. You take us to the other bank of the river."

The boatman did not seem to be in a hurry at all. He said in clear words: "Please wait for some time. I will not be able to hurry up. You will cross the river in no time. But my ancestors are waiting for ages to get liberation. With the water obtained by washing your lotus feet, I have to arrange the liberation of my ancestors first. Then you go to the other side."

The worried Ganga was satisfied now. The boatman is not troubling the Lord unnecessarily.

13

Lord's Name is Stronger than Lord

It is often said that the name of the Lord is more powerful than the Lord himself. One has to grow faith in God who is sitting in the *sanctum sanctorum* (viz. heart) of every living being and once the faith bridge is made, the grace of the Lord starts flowing. To establish such faith it is often said as an example that the devotee of Shri Ramachandra, Hanuman had crossed the sea by air by taking the name of the Lord, but when the Lord Shri Ramachandra himself wanted to cross the sea to go to Lanka He required a bridge to be constructed.

In this connection two incidents are often quoted which establish the strength of *japa*. While the bridge was being constructed to facilitate Lord Shri Ramachandra cross the sea an interesting incident happened. The Lord was watching from a distance that his devotees were bringing large chunks of mountain parts or stones and two of his devotees Nala and Nila were writing his name on the same and the stones were floating in the sea water. Thus piece by piece the bridge was getting constructed. The Lord was amused with such happening and now he wanted to test the same himself. He then lifted a small stone and threw the same in the water to see whether the same keeps floating. To his utter surprise He saw that the stone sank. He was himself surprised with the incident and he looked to his younger brother Lakshmana for the reason. Lakshmana smiled and replied: "Nothing wrong, when the stone was in your hand it was safe and the moment it got detatched it had to sink."

In another incident Vibhishana, the king of Lanka had written on a small piece of paper the name of the Lord (viz. Rama) and after folding the same, he had given it to somebody and told: "Now you can cross the sea. But do not open and see what is written on that paper. If you do so, you will sink." The man tied the paper in his cloth and was crossing the sea as told. But in the middle of the sea he wanted to know what was written on the paper. The moment he opened and read it, he sank.

The above stories bear a great value on the faith in the Almighty who is already staying inside all of us.

14

Bear No Malice

IT WAS THAT particular day when Lord Shri Ramachandra was due to arrive in Ayodhya after completion of fourteen years of exile in the forest. In the war the mighty Ravana was slayed and Vibhishana was installed on the throne of Lanka. Now the advance information of arrival had already been sent by Shri Rama through Hanuman and the life of Bharata had been saved with the news of arrival of Shri Rama within the scheduled period. To welcome Shri Ramachandra on the night of the new moon the city was illuminated with the flame of lamps in rows in all residences of Ayodhya. Even now on the day of the new moon in the month of Karttika the dwelling houses of Hindus are illuminated with rows of lighted lamps to remember the day of return of Lord Shri Ramachandra to Ayodhya and the same is celebrated as Dipavali.

The residents of Ayodhya had an intense desire to meet the Lord and everybody wished that Shri Rama should meet them first. When the Lord's carrier *pushpaka* chariot touched the ground of Ayodhya, He prostrated on the ground to show respect to the holy land of Ayodhya. The Lord satisfied the desire of the residents of Ayodhya of being met first by splitting himself into the equal number of forms (for individually meeting them) by giving the feeling that he met every individual before others. To satisfy every individual being of Ayodhya, this unique divine play was the proof of love for his devotees shown by the Lord.

The cordial meeting with the spiritual teacher, elders and younger brothers was also done in the right sequence. Everybody was thirsty to drink the nectar of grace of the Lord and after meeting him, all were satisfied upto the brim. Suddenly Shri Ramachandra saw that the mothers were standing ready for according ceremonial *arati* welcome with lighted lamps and auspicious articles. The formal welcome to the son was performed by mother Kaushalya followed by mother Sumitra. The same was repeated for Lakshmana and Sita also. Now Shri Ramachandra saw that mother Kaikeyi was conspicuously missing from the scene. After prostrating to and getting blessings from the mothers Kaushalya and Sumitra, the son Shri Ramachandra wanted to know why mother Kaikeyi was not there to welcome them? He was told that mother Kaikeyi had locked herself behind the closed doors of the palace since she considered herself responsible for their fourteen years of exile in the forest and the calamity faced by the daughter-in-law Sita. The Lord immediately walked down to the closed door in the palace and humbly requested the mother to come out.

Several requests made by the son remained unanswered since mother Kaikeyi had the opinion that her face was not worth showing since she had committed a sin. Now Shri Ramachandra adopted a novel method to end the deadlock. He said: "Mother! if you do not come out now we will go back to the forest again for fourteen years." This shock treatment worked and she responded immediately. Mother Kaikeyi came out concealing her weeping face behind the veil. Ramachandra said: "Mother! Your son is here awaiting a formal welcome and acceptance."

Mother Kaikeyi replied: "I shall accord a formal welcome to you, if you confirm that you have excused me from the sin I have committed."

To this the son said: "Mother! No son need excuse the mother. It is the mother only who excuses the son, always. Anything else if you ask, I shall try to give you."

Mother replied: "You promise that you will give."

Son said: "If it is possible for me, I shall definitely give it to you. I promise."

Mother now said: "You have given your word. I shall be convinced that you do not hold any malice against me, if you promise to come in my womb in your next birth."

On the condition imposed by mother Kaikeyi on him Shri Ramachandra smiled. Only a few moments earlier He had assured mother Kaushalya that at the next time of arrival in this world He would come into her arms as her son. He told mother Kaikeyi: "All right mother. I promise." Then the mother and the son met and both were seen shedding tears of joy. Mother Kaikeyi's guilt complex got washed out by the tears of joy of getting Shri Ramachandra as her own son in the next birth.

The words given by Narayana in *Treta-yuga* was complied with in *Dvapara-yuga* in totality. The wife of Vasudeva, Devaki was Kaikeyi in her previous birth and that is why Narayana came in the womb of Devaki and appeared on earth as Shri Krishna. He had kept the promise made to mother Kaushalya also by going in the arms of Yashoda, wife of Nanda of Braj. The mother Kaushalya in *Treta-yuga* had come again in *Dvapara-yuga* as Yashoda. See how tactfully Narayana kept his promises to both the mothers!

15

The Lord Knows no Enmity

A TOTAL GLOOM descended on Lanka. With the distressing news of the death of Meghanada, the mother Mandodari fainted and dropped on the floor and the condition of father King Ravana also was equally bad. Recovering from the shock Ravana called an emissary and sent a message to the enemy camp requesting for a cease fire on the next day since cremation of the body of the crown prince Meghanada is to be held.

The envoy reached the enemy camp with the message sent by King Ravana. He got the respect due to an envoy from the enemy camp. Shri Ramachandra in reply sent a message stating: "The proposal is being agreed to. If the ten-necked Ravana gives consent, I, Rama, the son of Kaushalya, along with my full team would like to be present at the time of cremation of the great valorous, Meghanada."

The proposal from the enemy camp got Ravana's assent. Shri Ramachandra along with his full team comprising Lakshmana, Hanuman, Jambavan and Sugriva went to Lanka and joined in Meghanada's funeral rites. At the moment of dying Meghanada had shouted: "Where is Lakshmana?" "Where is Ramachandra?" Only for this reason and being a treasurehouse of compassion, Shri Ramachandra went to the site of cremation to bestow emancipation to the brave Meghanada's soul.

The body of Meghanada was consigned to flames and was reduced to ashes. Suddenly, a gust of wind blew and the ashes of the body of Meghanada collected at the lotus-feet of Lord Shri Ramachandra. Even if an enemy takes the name of Lord Sri Rama at the time of his death, the lord will bless his soul with permanent peace.

16

Devotion is More Important than Ritual

THE RAMAVAT *ASHRAMA* on the bank of river Beas had been an ideal place for meditation and learning since the surrounding atmosphere was without the usual pollution and disturbance of a big township. The *ashrama* was run by a very learned person who was known to everybody as Guruji. The number of persons living in the *ashrama* was very limited since the admission to the *ashrama* was granted by Guruji judiciously. Apart from his knowledge, Guruji was also very compassionate with the students and everybody used to get father's love from Guruji.

One morning Guruji was taking his mandatory bath in the river to prepare himself for the worship of the presiding deity Shri Ramachandra. Suddenly he saw a boy of fragile structure sitting under a tree. The boy looked desolate. A boy at that odd hour sitting alone raised questions in the mind of Guruji. He hurriedly finished his bath and asked the boy: "Who are you?, What is your problem?" Answers given by the boy revealed that he is an orphan with no place to live in. The compassionate Guruji asked the boy whether he would like to go along with him and live in the *ashrama*. The boy bluntly asked: "What do I get by going there?" Guruji replied: "You get shelter, food and work in the *ashrama*." The boy agreed to go to the *ashrama* with Guruji with the condition that he will get food to satisfy his hunger.

Within a short period it was proved that the boy whose name was Ahriya was an excellent worker and was very obedient to all. There rose a question also in keeping him in the *ashrama* since Ahriya consumed food meant for three persons at one time. Guruji being very compassionate did not like to lose the boy due to his merits. Thus, Ahriya remained happily in the *ashrama* and worked day long to keep everyone happy.

A peculiar problem arose on *ekadashi* day when the residents of the *ashrama* were required to observe a fast. Ahriya protested and refused to go without food on that day. Guruji had initiated the boy and hence following the *ashrama* rules it was mandatory. But, considering the tender age of the boy Guruji agreed to his taking food on the day but with the condition that he will have to cook the food outside the boundary of the *ashrama* and eat there after offering some to the presiding deity of the *ashrama*. The store of the *ashrama* was ordered to give sufficient flour and vegetables to Ahriya for cooking.

He walked down with the provisions and chose a desolate place under a tree for cooking the food. He did not have difficulty in arranging firewood from nearby locations. The food was cooked well and the only process left was to consume the same to satisfy his gluttonous hunger. But he remembered the instructions given by Guruji that the food has to be offered to Lord Rama before eating. Ahriya served the food on a leaf properly cleaned and sat with his eyes closed to observe the rules of offering to the Lord. When Ahriya opened his eyes he was surprised to see that a person of dark hue, yellow raiment and with bow and arrows on his shoulder was sitting in front of the food offered to Shri Rama and eating the same. Ahriya got very angry and asked: "Who are you?, Why are you eating the food offered to Shri Rama?" The person smiled and said: "I am eating the food offered to me only. I am Ramachandra." Ahriya saw that all the food cooked by him had vanished, and there was none left for him — he had to go without food; in other words he observed a fast by compulsion.

On the second *ekadashi* day Ahriya wanted to play safe and he demanded double the ration. The cooked food was offered to Shri Rama. But this time along with Shri Rama, a woman was easting the food. He was told that she was Sita the wife of Shri Rama. There was no food left for him, and he had to fast the second time also.

On the third *ekadashi* day, three people — Shri Rama, Sita and Lakshmana — ate all the food cooked by him with three times the quantity of ration, and he had to go without food a third time as well.

On the fourth *ekadashi* day as well he could not eat as there was none left for him after four persons Shri Rama, Sita, Lakshmana and Hanuman ate all the food cooked by him with four times the quantity of materials.

The fifth *ekadashi* arrived and Ahriya demanded

ration equal to five times the usual quantity. This time Ahriya was extra careful. He did not cook the food, and offered the uncooked materials to the presiding deity of the hermitage. He had closed his eyes for invocation and other rituals. When he opened his eyes he saw that this time in addition to four persons, two more had come. On enquiry, he learned that they are the Guru-couple of Shri Ramachandra, known as Lord Shiva and Goddess Parvati. This time Shri Ramachandra said "My dear devotee! This time we shall cook the food and distribute." Shri Lakshmana brought the firewood and Sita Devi cooked the food. When the cooking was done, Shri Ramachandra formally offered the food to his Guru Shiva-Parvati in the same way as Ahriya did.

Shri Ramachandra asked Sita Devi to distribute the food. Everybody sat in a line and the place decided for Ahriya was the last one. Before distribution of the food Shri Ramachandra told something in the ear of Sita Devi. After distribution of the food Ahriya saw that he has been given only a small portion of the food. He got angry and said: "I won't eat. I shall observe *ekadashi*." When everybody present persuaded Ahriya, he took that small quantity of food and what a surprise, his hunger was satiated, his stomach was full and he felt as if he had taken a sumptuous meal.

Then he rose from his seat and prostrated before everybody and said: "All of you please wait here for some time. I shall run to the hermitage and come back with my *guruji*."

When the Guru came to the place, he saw that six persons were sitting under a tree. When he recognized all of them he prostrated before them and thanked them for blessing his disciple, Ahriya, by eating the food offered by him with devotion.

With humility the Guruji said: "My Ahriya! I do not know whether I have given you anything, but today I shall thank you for something you have done. Because of you only, I could see the Almighty with my own eyes. I have understood that *ekadashi,* does not mean fasting alone; the essential thing is to love the divine from the core of the heart. Without absolute devotion observing *ekadashi* has no meaning."

17

Faith in God Does Wonders

THIS GIGANTIC DAM was constructed during the British rule since a large part of the land in south India was suffering due to floods in the river Krishna. It took a lot of expertise and supervision of overseas experts for quite a long time to construct this dam in the basin of river Krishna. There had been teething troubles during testing and commissioning of this project and actually the same had threatened the reputation of design and construction personnel even. When on the third attempt the dam again gave way against the water pressure during peak rainy season, the chief of the project was even taunted about his capability by the higher management. Hence, Wilson was anxious to prove his expertise during the approaching fourth trial during the peak monsoon.

On that day the expert was walking along the bank of the river thinking deeply of the various design and construction modifications undertaken after the third failure. He walked quite a long distance to a place he had not visited earlier. There he saw a cottage in which a pious man was doing prayers before some idols — Rama, Sita, Lakshmana and Hanuman. The pious man asked Wilson what the problem was and what brought him to the cottage. When Wilson explained his problems, the man said "Have faith in God, and do your duty sincerely. God will definitely bless you with success." Wilson prayed to God, in his own way, before the idols, and went back to his camp.

There was a heavy downpour in the night, and Wilson feared that the rain water flowing in the dam would breach the embankment. He did not know what to do in the circumstances. He thought that only god should help him. He prayed sincerely for divine assistance. Wilson was unable to keep himself behind the doors in his camp. He put on his rain coat and gumboots and went to the site to physically inspect the portion of the dam under threat. When he reached the spot he got panic-stricken to see that the dam was overflowing and might burst at any time.

In the terrible downpour the expert stood dumbstruck for a long period alone. Suddenly, there was a thunderclap and in the flash of light he saw two young men standing on the dam bund pointing their bows and arrows at the waves of water striking the dam with unusual force. Wilson wondered who those persons could be who were standing guard at the site where he feared the dam would break. Suddenly it struck him that the two persons resembled the two male idols in the cottage he happened to visit and in which he prayed for a moment. In the morning he inspected the site and was happy and relieved to see that the dam did not burst and it was safe. He went to the cottage and narrated the night's happenings to the pious man.

The pious man heard the full incident from the new devotee and prostrated before the idol of Lord Shri Rama.

The pious man told Wilson, "Your faith in Shri Rama is greater and more sincere than mine, that is why you could see the Lord and his brother with your own eyes, which I could not, even after worshipping the Lord for so many years. Only Rama and Lakshmana saved the dam from bursting and causing havoc to thousands of people living in the area."

The dam stands erect even now surviving the torrents of the mighty river year after year by the grace of Lord Shri Rama. As a gesture of gratitude for the divine help, Wilson generously donated cash and gold to the pious man — now a temple stands at the site of the cottage as a testimony to the faith of a foreigner in Shri Rama. The presiding deity in the temple is called. "Iri Kattha Raman" — Rama who saved the Lake.

Note : This is a true story.

18

Universe within God

INFANTILE SPORTS of Lord Shri Krishna at Gokula had been of great interest to the devotees from time immemorial. Out of such incidents one is of the infant Lord's eating earth. The incident was witnessed by the Lord's elder brother Balarama and the same got reported to mother Yashoda for action. This time the culprit was presented to the mother by Balarama along with other cowherd boys. The allegation was taken quite seriously and the Lord's mother lifted up a stick to punish the culprit on the spot. As per normal practice the accused was asked to confirm whether the crime has been committed or not. It was a difficult situation. If crime is accepted, then punishment is imminent, and if it is denied the elder brother Balarama may be reprimanded. As such, the infant replied: "why don't you see it with your own eyes?" When the mother peeped inside the open mouth of the infant, she saw the whole universe inside, and got terribly upset by the sight. She forgot to reprimand the infant and ran to her husband Nanda to report. Nanda heard every bit of the incident and replied: "You are getting aged. You might have seen something else!"

In the eyes of the infant Shri Krishna, the father Nanda was a person without firm belief in his divinity.

But why should the father be deprived of a similar divine sight by the son? As such, the incident was made to happen in a different way. The father Nanda was a confirmed Vaishnava (viz. follower of Lord Vishnu). He was worshipping *shaligrama* stone (viz. taken as an emblem of Lord Vishnu) daily after bathing in Yamuna. The *shaligrama shila* was worshipped with one thousand and eight *tulasi* leaves after dipping the same in sandal paste, accompanied by utterance of thousand and eight names of Lord Vishnu. One day the father Nanda was about to start the worship and the infant Lord (Shri Krishna) landed on the spot.

Child Nandalal watched the bathing process of the *shaligrama shila* with immense pleasure. Then the offering of sandal paste-dipped *tulasi* leaves with the thousand and eight names of Lord Vishnu started. The *shaligrama* was disappearing below the heaps of *tulasi* leaves frequently and the father Nanda was recovering the stone everytime for fresh offering. The child was really enjoying the disappearance and reappearance of the *shaligrama shila* under the heaps of *tulasi* leaves. Now it was time for offering cooked food to the deity. Mother Yashoda confirmed from the kitchen that the food was ready. Father Nanda got up to bring the cooked food from the kitchen and while going asked Nandalal to see that nobody disturbs the deity during his absence. Nandalal ensured with a broad smile that the necessary guarding will be done.

Father Nanda returned within a short time with the cooked food from the kitchen. The ritual of offering the food to the deity started. Father Nanda got busy in recovering the *shaligrama* stone from the heaps of *tulasi* leaves. In the first attempt he could not locate the deity, hence he started searching again. But when he could not locate the deity after several attempts he became restless. Nandalal was asked whether anybody came to the spot in his absence, to which Nandalal gestured "no" by nodding his head. Suddenly the father discovered that Nandalal was not talking. When Nanda looked at the child he found that the right side of the child's face was swollen. Nanda suspected some mischief and asked Nandalal to open his mouth. When he looked inside he started shivering. He saw the entire universe inside the child's mouth, including himself, Nandalal and the *puja mandapa*. Seeing the supernatural scene inside the mouth of Nandalal, Nanda remembered what Yashoda had said some time back. As such, Nanda ran to his wife Yashoda to tell her about the wonderful vision. Yashoda heard everything and teased him: "You are getting old. You might have seen something else."

When Nanda came back to the *puja mandapa* he saw that the *shaligrama shila* was back in its original position to accept the offerings of the devotee. By the *lila* of *maya* both Nanda and Yashoda forgot the divine vision instantaneously and showed their parental love towards Nandalal, the god in human form.

19

Enjoy the Lord's Lila

THE FRIEND brought the news that his mother at home is going to make *laddu*s. Kanhai was also told that his friend is extremely sorry since his mother does not give him more than two *laddu*s. Kanhai told his friend that if he does as suggested by Him, he will get four *laddu*s that day. The necessary plans were made.

Now Kanhai arrived at the kitchen where the *laddu*s were being made. The preparation was at the finishing stage and Kanhai sat there without being asked. His untimely arrival made the mistress uncomfortable and worried too. Kanhai on his own started conversation in his customary indistinct dialect. Now the time arrived for enacting the drama. Suddenly, some loud weeping was heard outside. The mistress recognized the weeping as her son's. The intensity of the noise was increasing and the mistress wanted to go outside the house to enquire. But the main problem was the presence of Kanhai in front of the *laddu*s. Ultimately the mistress left the place giving Kanhai the charge of guarding the house.

Now the stage was free and Kanhai started eating the delicious *laddu*s along with his friends who were hiding behind the windows. Kanhai, however, saved four *laddus* for his friend who was the main actor.

Then Kanhai came out of the front door of the house with those four *laddus*. When the actor friend saw that Kanhai had come with the booty, instead of weeping he started smiling. The sudden change of atmosphere puzzled the mistress of the house and she ran inside to check, particularly the *laddus*. She saw that the platter was empty and the *laddus* had gone. She could very well understand the conspiracy hatched for robbing the *laddus*.

When Kanhai was asked about the missing *laddus*, he "innocently" replied that he was asked to only look after the house; the house is fully secure, and so he should not be questioned about anything else. The mistress now saw her son standing at a distance holding four *laddus* in his hand. She felt happy and honoured at having witnessed of *lila* of Kanhai, the darling of Nandgaon.

20

The Lord is the Stealer of Hearts

THEFT OF BUTTER and cream of milk had become a regular feature in Braj Village. The women of the village tried several methods to protect the butter and cream from being stolen. A woman adopted a novel method.

After preparation of the product the same was kept in a clay pot hung from the ceiling by strings. The pot was covered by a clay plate and a little water was kept on the plate. The idea behind such a device was that if somebody tried to remove the plate, the water contained on it would pour down. To ensure additional safety the mistress laid her cot below the hanging pot to enjoy her afternoon nap. She was sure that nobody could pilfer the butter without her notice.

The news of such fool-proof security for the milk products reached little Krishna. A counter action was immediately planned.

The leader along with two hefty associates entered the operation theatre after ensuring that the mistress lying down below was fast asleep. The leader used his associates to go up to the level of the lid on the hanging pot. Now with the help of a lotus-stalk the water on the plate was drained to the floor level without a drop spilling on the mistress sleeping down below. Removal of plate and the pot followed without disturbing anybody. After collecting the booty the group left the place silently.

The mistress *gopi* was comfortably sleeping since she was satisfied that the security for the materials was flawless. When she woke up and stepped on the floor she found that the floor was totally wet. With anxiety she looked up and was dumbfounded to find that the butter pot was missing. She also found some things also missing. The boy of swarthy hue had taken her heart and mind also along with the butter and cream of milk.

21

Devotee's Concern for Lord's Comforts

VRINDAVANA BEING the holy place connected with divine acts by Lord Shri Krishna is full of temples built by devotees of the Vaishnava cult. The temple of Biharilalji is one of such temples which attracts devotees due to its size and grandeur. The priest Hariji was a very respected person and people used to assemble at the temple to witness the love and affection of the priest towards the presiding deity Biharilalji or Nandlal. Hariji remained attached to the Lord from the very morning hours. The glamour and beauty of the temple also was appreciated by devotees from far and wide. At night Hariji used to keep four laddus in a silver casket near the bed of Biharilalji with the idea that if Biharilalji felt hungry during the night time, he could eat those. The main temple was at a raised level and devotees had to go twenty steps up to have a glimpse of Biharilalji.

One night while closing the doors of the bedroom of Biharilalji, the priest forgot to put the sweetmeat. The temple had a sweetmeat shop at the ground level a little away from the entry point of the steps to go up. The owner of the shop was keeping the shop open up to midnight to prepare fresh sweetmeats for selling to devotees visiting the temple in the morning hours for offering the same to the deity.

That night the owner was thinking of closing the shop since it was already midnight. No sound could be heard from anywhere since everybody was fast asleep. Suddenly he saw that a boy of swarthy complexion had come to his shop. The confectioner could not remember where he had seen the boy earlier. He thought that the customer must have come from one of the houses situated in the vicinity. The boy asked the shop owner for four *laddus*. Fresh *laddus* were available and the same were given to the customer. He asked the customer: "My son! From which house have you come? Tell me that only. In the morning I shall take the price for the *laddus*." The boy showed the direction where the Biharilalji's temple stood. The boy suddenly removed one of the bangles from his wrist and asked the confectioner to take that as the price. When the shop-keeper did not agree to take the bangle as the price of just four *laddus* the boy threw the bangle inside the shop and disappeared on the steps of the Biharilalji's temple in the dark. In the darkness of the night the shop owner could not locate the bangle. He decided to search for the same the next morning and went home after closing the shop.

At daybreak the priest Hariji came to the temple to perform the morning rituals. The first of such rituals was to go to the bedroom of Biharilalji and wake him up lovingly. Hariji looked with affection at Nandalal on the bed. When Hariji made all preparations for dressing up the deity, he found that the bangle on the left wrist was not in its place. He clearly remembered that when he had put Biharilalji on bed the previous night, the golden bangle was very much on his left wrist. Hariji was sure that the misplaced bangle would definitely be found on the bed but he became nervous when the costly golden bangle could not be located. He was getting late to open the main door of the temple since a number of people had already assembled behind the closed door. Without the bangles, it was not possible to put Biharilalji on the cradle since the devotees would detect the same the moment they looked at the deity. An intensive search also could not solve the problem, and the priest was in tears thinking of the repercussions since he was answerable to the authorities for the valuable material which was missing.

People waiting outside started getting impatient and the absence of the golden bangle from the left wrist of Biharilalji was reported to them as theft at night in the temple. As such people started leaving the site without the early morning *darshana* of Biharilalji. Comments of the public about the incident were unfavourable for the priest particularly.

When the visitors were returning displeased they told the shop owner also about the missing bangle. The news was not favourable for the confectioner also since that would have an impact on the sale of *laddus*. Suddenly the shop owner remembered that somebody at midnight had come to him for *laddus* and wanted to pay by giving a bangle. He also remembered that the visitor had thrown the bangle inside his shop when he did not like to take the cost in that way. As such he started searching for the bangle inside the shop. Within a short time the bangle could be retrieved. He saw that the bangle was golden and looked to be quite costly. The thought flashed in his mind that the bangle could be the same one which was reported to be missing from the temple.

Within a short time the sweetmeat shop owner was with the priest of the temple. The priest was thanking him since the bangle was the same, reported lost. But when the description of the nocturnal visitor was communicated to Hariji, he started shedding tears continuously. The sweetmeat shop owner was trying to convince that he had no role in the reported theft of the bangle but the priest was shedding tears for some other reason. Suddenly, Hariji got up to check on something. He hurriedly went to the bed of Nandalalji and saw that small pieces of *laddu*s were strewn on the bed. But what surprised the priest was that the silver container in which the *laddu*s were normally placed before Biharilalji was not on the small table. Hariji again started weeping when he did find the same inside the locked almirah. With tearful eyes the priest said: "It was my fault. I did not keep the *laddu*s for Biharilalji last night by mistake. He must have felt hungry at the dead of night. He must have gone to the shop himself to get *laddu*s. Since he did not carry money with him he had paid the price by throwing the bangle inside the shop."

The confectioner could not understand about whom the priest was talking. He could only hear the priest speaking to him: "My obeisance to you. You could see him in person whereas I could not even after worshipping him for so many years." The puzzle was not solved for the shop owner. He was left wondering whether he would, or would not, be cleared of any role in the reported theft of the bangle.

22

Be Firm in Your Commitment

VRINDAVANA SWAMI had been known to others as an ardent Vaishnava mendicant. He had come to Vrindavana long back to live on the dust which had the rare fortune of getting the physical touch of the lotus-feet of Lord Shri Krishna. Poverty had been the Swami's constant companion. He however had the company of Damodara whom he had worshipped and served as the Lord. Without offering to Damodara he would not take anything for himself.

In Vrindavana there existed institutions which supply food daily to poor persons as charity. These institutions played a major role in feeding the mendicants who spend their lives in meditation on the Lord. Vrindavana Swami also lived quite happily on the food supplied by a particular institution.

One day when he had gone to the institution to collect the food, he heard that distribution would be delayed due to some reason. When he was waiting for the food he suddenly remembered that Lord Damodara at his residence would be waiting to be fed. So, he hurriedly went home and offered him sugar-candy and water. After that he again went to the charitable institution to collect the food when distributed. That day the distribution of *bhoga* could be done only by the late evening. With that food Vrindavana came home and started to eat the same since Damodara had been given food already, earlier in the day. He decided that offering the *bhoga* to Damodara was not required.

But as soon as he had put a morsel of food inside his mouth Vrindavana thought that his action was inappropriate since without first offering to Damodara he had never taken anything till that time. The *prasada* becomes *mahaprasada* only after it is offered to Damodara and the food in his mouth was not *mahaprasada* that day. As such the food could not be eaten since that would lead to committing a sin. But to take out the *prasada* or spit it from the mouth was also a great sin. As such Vrindavana was in a dilemma. No apparent solution could be thought of by him.

To save him from the dilemma Vrindavana submitted himself to Lord Damodara and started praying for help. He was praying continuously and fell on the ground. His body became weak and his mouth remained open. In that condition three nights passed. In that semi-conscious condition he could make out that somebody was calling him. With great difficulty he opened his eyes and saw that the neighbours were calling his name and were trying to bring him back to the normal state. From them he learned that a boy of swarthy complexion had come a short while ago, and that he ate something taken out from the Swami's open mouth. When the boy was leaving the place, he had informed the neighbours that Vrindavana had fallen sick and they should take care of him.

Now Vrindavana was shedding tears of joy. He understood that Lord Damodara Himself had come and had taken the *prasada* from his mouth to make the same *mahaprasada*. He could not see the Lord with his own eyes but indeed the touch of the Lord is no small achievement for a human being.

23

Find Truth in Falsehood

ONCE THE GOPIS of Vrindavana famous for the divine acts of Lord Shri Krishna wanted to serve the sage Durvasa with milk products but their problem was the soaring river Yamuna. The milk products (viz. butter, curd, *khira,* and cream) had to be taken to the hermitage of the revered sage situated on the other side of the river. The devotees requested Lord Shri Krishna to help. The Lord said: "Tell Yamuna that if it is true that the Kanhaiya had not touched a woman in his life, the river should give way to the other side." The *gopi*s knew that this can never be true as Lord Shri Krishna's dalliance with the cowherd girls of Braj is well known. However, left with no other option, *gopi*s repeated the sentence to the river Yamuna and to their surprise Yamuna parted into two and gave them the way to go to the other side.

With the milk products the *gopi*s served and worshipped the revered sage Durvasa and the sage was very pleased with the *gopi*s' devotion. Now the cowherdesses wanted to return to their homes but there was the huge river Yamuna to be crossed. Krishna is not with them to help. So they told their problem to sage Durvasa. The sage started laughing and said: "Tell

Yamuna that if it is true that Durvasa is always fasting, she should give passage to you to return to the other side of the river." This was another plain lie. The sage ate every bit of milk products in front of the *gopis*' eyes and the statement that he is ever fasting is far from true. Again riding on a swing of distrust the *gopis* repeated sage Durvasa's words to Yamuna who readily parted and gave access to the *gopis* to return to their homes.

The *gopis* were still wondering how it was true that Kanhaiya has not touched a woman in His Life and that Sage Durvasa is ever fasting after consuming so much of food in front of them! When the question was put to Lord Shri Krishna, He smiled at the devotees and said "Soul has no connection with gender and sages consume food as oblation into the sacrificial fire, hence they are ever fasting."

24

Cunningness is a Part of Warfare

MATHURA WAS about to be invaded by the monarch Jarasandha for the eighteenth time. A new problem cropped up in the form of Kalayavana who suddenly attacked Mathura with a very large and strong army. Lord Shri Krishna sensed danger at the prospect of fighting against two strong foes — Jarasandha and Kalayavana — at the same time.

The matter was discussed with Lord Balarama, the elder brother of Lord Shri Krishna. They decided to build a city elsewhere for all the people of Mathura to live in. The architect of gods, Vishvakarma was asked to construct a fortress in the western sea. The fortress was made over an area of ninety square miles with a city inside. The city was extremely beautiful and in the centre of the city stood the palaces belonging to the rulers of Yadus, Ugrasena and Vasudeva, Balarama and Shri Krishna. The city was named Dwaraka. Lord Shri Krishna transferred Mathura along with its inhabitants to the new city by dint of His supernatural power. Lord Balarama was left back with some soldiers to take care of the city of Mathura.

Now a peculiar divine *lila* was played by Shri Krishna who is known as the dispeller of agony of his devotees. He appeared at the lion gate of Mathura wearing a garland of lotus and without any weapon to face Kalayavana. The Lord with the hue of water-laden cloud was looking attractive in His yellow silk attire and brilliantly shiny Kaustubha gem. He was endowed with four massive long arms. He was lotus eyed. His face showed abundance of joy resembling a full blown lotus. His ears had brilliant alligator shaped earrings. His garland was making Him more beautiful.

Kalayavana saw Him. Since the figure of the person coming out of the lion gate tallied with the description given by the celestial sage Narada, Kalayavana identified him as the Vasudeva whom he was looking for. When he saw that Vasudeva was without a weapon he also wanted to face him without carrying a weapon with him. Kalayavana was surprised to see that having seen him coming, the Lord started running away with his back turned against him. As such, he also started chasing the Lord. In this way the Lord started his *lila* as Ranchoda (viz. the fleeing Lord from the battlefield). In this divine sport the Lord sometimes came near the enemy giving the impression that he has been caught, to keep the enemy trying to catch him up. While chasing Krishna Kalayavana also shouted several times that he was trying to run away from the battlefield though born as a Yadu. The Lord did not reply to him and tactfully pulled him inside a dark mountain cave.

On entering the dark cave Kalayavana found a person sleeping on the floor. He thought it must be Vasudeva only who was trying to save himself by pretending that he was sleeping. He kicked the sleeping person. The person who was sleeping there was somebody else. The person woke up and slowly opened his eyes when he came up on his feet. He looked around to see the person who had the courage to kick him. His angry look fell on Kalayavana and he was reduced to ashes instantaneously.

Some information is necessary about this sleeping person, who had the power to burn anybody on just opening his eyes with anger if he is disturbed in his sleep. The name of the person was Mucukunda, son of Mandhata in the family of Ikshvaku. Mucukunda was a great king and he was a great warrior also. He was entrusted with the job of saving the gods, when the demons were playing havoc. When the gods got Karttikeya as their army chief, they wanted to reward Mucukunda for the marvellous service rendered. Since nobody of his time existed, he wanted rest for a long time. Gods had told him: "We can give you anything except liberation which only the imperishable Lord Vishnu can give." Mucukunda was a person of great renown. Hence he asked: "I am extremely tired, I require a long sound sleep. Grant me a long slumber." The boon was granted with an additional clause: "Anybody who awakens you thoughtlessly in the middle of your sleep shall instantaneously be reduced to ashes when seen by you." Kalayavana became a victim of that additional clause.

Now Shri Krishna (Lord Vishnu) appeared before Mucukunda and gave his blessing.

Lord Shri Krishna with his elder brother Balarama had thereafter destroyed the entire army of Kalayavana.

25

Remain Unattached to Surroundings

FATHER VEDAVYASA wanted to know whether his son Shukadeva was endowed with the knowledge of *Brahman* ever since birth. As such he instructed his son Shukadeva to visit King Janaka. The instruction of the father was given due respect and Shukadeva arrived at the gate of the royal court of King Janaka at Mithila.

The ascetic Shukadeva did not receive a good reception at the palace. The security personnel did not allow Shukadeva in without prior permission from the monarch. Shukadeva was told that getting approval for entry to the royal court was a time-consuming affair and he had to wait at the gate only. It took three days to get permission of entry from King Janaka. The sage was somewhat dissatisfied with this treatment.

Sage Shukadeva was informed that King Janaka had agreed to meet him in the royal court in the midst of other people. Shukadeva had expected that the King of Mithila would meet him in person in seclusion. The messenger took Shukadeva to the entry point of the royal court and left him there. Shukadeva could hear the loud noises from a distance only. On entry to the royal court he found that the court was crowded beyond imagination. On the throne, the King of Mithila Janaka was sitting and enjoying the entertainments. A group of beautiful women were dancing and presentation of songs was accompanied by the instruments played very loud. Sage Shukadeva started feeling somewhat uncomfortable with the atmosphere. In his opinion the same suited worldly people and not King Janaka who was known to be firmly established in the knowledge of *Brahman,* and a combination of both was not possible.

Suddenly, sage Shukadeva saw that King Janaka was gesturing him to take a seat. Self-abnegator Shukadeva sat down, remembering the instructions given by his father. He however, still maintained his firm opinion that keeping immersed in the sea of royal luxury is not desirable. The scene remained unchanged for a long time. He was watching King Janaka with astonishment. At last he saw that the Royal Ascetic was asking him to to go near him. The moment sage Shukadeva went near, the Royal Ascetic Janaka said: "I know you, and I also know why you have come to meet me. I am giving you a cup filled up to the brim with oil. Kindly circumambulate the royal court with the cup in your hand. You are to ensure that even a drop of oil does not fall on the way."

Shukadeva could not follow the real purpose behind such instructions by the Royal Ascetic. However, he took the cup in his hands and went round in the chaotic condition of the royal court. He could fulfil the condition stated by King Janaka and not a drop of oil fell on the way. When he came back to the Royal Ascetic Janaka, he praised him for the success. He said: "O great sage. Now tell me, when you were passing through the royal court with this cup of oil filled up to the brim, did you know that a noisy celebration was going on in this royal court?" Sage Shukadeva replied: "I did not hear anything."

The Royal Ascetic Janaka smiled and said: "You are a real knower of *Brahman*. The saint Vedavyasa had already come to know about this fact. Your father is anxiously waiting for your return."

The holder of knowledge of *Brahman, brahmagyani* Shukadeva looked at the Raja-rishi Janaka, with wonder. He was happy that he had seen a person who was lonely and calm even in the din of noises in the court.

26

Mind Often Makes Fickle Judgements

THE INCIDENT took place in a small township bordering the desert in Rajasthan. It was midday time during the fierce summer when a hot sandstorm was blowing. The angry desert had openly challenged humanity. The residents of the township were hiding themselves behind the closed doors and windows.

A wayfarer was walking through the lane having multi-storied buildings on both sides. He was very thirsty and was in search of accommodation for himself. No door or window was open and hence he was loudly asking for drinking water from the residents. Nobody was responding, and he pronouned the judgement: "Stone-hearted wicked people."

Suddenly, one of the windows on the third floor of a multi-storey building opened. The wayfarer saw that he was being told to wait. A pleasant, but loud, voice reached him: "Friend! wait there, I shall get you drinking water." The judge changed the verdict: "Persons are large-hearted, magnanimous."

The wayfarer waited in the lane only. A long time passed but nobody came with the water. He thought: "Why was I asked to wait? If I had gone further I could have got drinking water." His judgement changed: "A liar." The generous person became a liar within a few minutes.

He started walking. He had gone only a few yards, when he heard somebody calling him from the back. He returned to the spot where he had been waiting earlier. The same person who had asked him to wait from the third-floor window was now standing at the entrance to the building. When the wayfarer came near, the person said apologetically: "Friend! I am sorry, I took a little extra time." I thought: "How could I give only water to a thirsty person on a hot day. Hence, I had gone to prepare sherbet for you. Please take this. You will definitely like it." The judge again changed the verdict: "Not a simple person. He is an *avatara*."

27

Do Not Concentrate on Life Only

SAINT DADUDAYAL was one of the celebrated ascetics. For his livelihood he had to accept the job of keeping accounts. He was kept tied to his job until the balance sheet was completed everyday.

That day it was raining badly. With the permission of the employer he had brought all note books home to complete the job. He was confused about an entry which was incorrect in the books. It looked as if somebody was playing foul with the simple-natured ascetic. The entrance door to the house was wide open and saint Dadudayal did not even notice that. It was raining continuously but the ascetic who was concentrating on his work did not even know that a few hours had passed. Suddenly, the mistake was detected and the whole struggle to tally the accounts came to an end. Saint Dadudayal's attention then got diverted and he saw it was raining heavily outside. As he looked up he saw that his *guruji* standing at his doorstep fully drenched in the rain.

Dadudayal said: "Guruji! Why are you standing in the rain outside? How long have you been standing there?"

Guruji replied: "Son! I am standing here for the last

two hours. I was watching you working on some accounts job very intently and you were engrossed so deeply in it!" The disciple asked: "Why did you not call me?"

Guruji replied: "If I had disturbed you, I could not have seen and enjoyed your meditative posture. I was only waiting for your attention for the last two hours, but the Almighty is waiting for you from time immemorial — He is just waiting for you to look at him and call him."

28

Do Not Follow Customs Blindly

IN THAT *ASHRAMA* students used to come from distant places to stay and study at the feet of the wise *guruji*. The knowledge gained during the course of stay in that *ashrama* was considered to be of great value. The daily routine included meditation, learning manners, study of Vedas and instructions from *guruji* to be followed by the disciples.

Once the arrival of a cat at the time of meditation created problems. The cat used to mew and jump on the lap of *guruji* creating disturbance. *Guruji* has a soft corner for animals, and so at the time of meditation to avoid disturbance from the cat, *guruji* made a rule to tie the cat to a tree of and keep milk before it. Thus, tying the cat to the tree at the time of meditation became a daily ritual or custom in the *ashrama*.

One day *guruji* left this world due to old age and the *ashrama* became rudderless. The senior-most among the disciples took charge of the *ashrama* to set things right. Since *guruji* was no more the facilities availed by the cat including the milk stopped abruptly. The cat also disappeared from the scene as it did not get any food at the *ashrama*. Now with the new leader on the seat, the disciples sat for meditation but even after repeated trials they could not meditate as they felt that something was amiss. Suddenly, they remembered that the customary ritual of tying the cat to the tree had not been done. So they caught hold of another cat and tied it to a tree at the time of meditation. But nobody could meditate properly because the new cat did not like being tied to a tree and wanted to be free, and therefore, it went on mewing and wailing when being tied, and did not drink any milk. Moreover, the new *guruji* did not like cats. Then the disciples realised that they should not stick to customs and rituals blindly and that customs are to be changed according to changed circumstances.

29

Bhakti and Gyana Lead to the Same Goal

TWO ARDENT DEVOTEES were living in close physical proximity in Janakpuri with diverse opinions about the worship of the Almighty. Dancer Ratna believed that the way preached by Mirabai was the right way to appease the Lord (*bhakti marga*) whereas Baba Narahari believed that the path of gaining knowledge by reading scriptures and extolling with rituals (*gyana marga*) was the ideal way.

Ratna was young and was quite an expert in singing and dancing. Every evening she was dancing before the deity and singing devotional songs to please the Almighty. She was sincere in showing her love and affection to the Lord during the performance and was sometimes lost in ecstasy and overwhelmed with emotion. Her intense devotion was admired by the people and slowly the number of people gathering at the temple every evening increased. Ratna had earned the reputation of a devotee of higher grade.

Baba Narahari had a small *ashrama* near the temple. Every evening a large number of people used to gather to hear the reading of the scriptures by the ascetic and to listen to his lectures and words of wisdom. The sound of music and dance at Ratna's temple in the evening was disturbing the serious atmosphere of Baba Narahari's *ashrama,* and was also attracting the people there. Within a short time the number of persons attending the evening prayers at Baba Narahari's *ashrama* dwindled, and the loss in numbers became a gain at Ratna's temple.

Baba Narahari believed that the *madhura-bhava* adopted by Ratna is not approved by the scriptures since the same is difficult to maintain and often leads to a person's downfall. The ascetic's main worry was that he was fast losing popularity and thereby financial earnings for the *ashrama.* Hence, one day he went personally to Ratna's temple and ordered that she should stop her music and dance since the same is causing pollution in the surroundings.

Ratna accepted the Baba's advice as the will of God and stopped her practice. She however, wanted to show her love to the Lord by donating a golden diadem to the deity in the temple. When the diadem was offered to the Lord, the Baba, out of spite and jealousy, said that the diadem should be kept on Lord Jagannath's head only if he bends down to receive it.

The temple priest kept the diadem at the feet of the deity, closed the door for the night and went home along with the Baba, Ratna and the other devotees. All were anxious to see what would happen next. Throughout the night Ratna did not sleep and was praying to her Lord with devotion.

The day dawned, and a huge crowd was waiting at the temple gate. When the priest after praying to Lord Jagannath opened the door to the *sanctum sanctorum*, he and all the devotees present were surprised to see that the diadem was on the Lord's head and that the Lord's head also looked slightly bent as if he had bowed to receive the crown. The Baba, with tears rolling down, fell at the feet of Ratna and asked for her pardon saying that he belittled her *bhakti marga* thinking that his own *gyana marga* was surperior in reaching to God, and that he now realized that both the paths lead towards the same goal.

30

True Devotees Know no Caste

DEVOTEES EVEN NOW have a feeling of thrill and ecstasy during their visit to Dakshineswara near Kolkata when they remember that the principal deity of the temple Mother Bhavatarini even breathed when she was worshipped by Thakur Shri Ramakrishna. As such she is known as the living goddess by the devotees. The most interesting fact remains that the place bears the purity of the touch of Ganga, Mother Kali and Thakur at the same time.

We come to the period when Thakur Shri Ramakrishna was no longer in a mortal body and many of his close associates visited the holy place for meditation and remembrance of the great soul. Against a question by somebody, an answer was given by a very close associate of the Thakur: "I visit Dakshinesvara to charge my batteries since every particle of that place bears the physical touch of Thakur." Rasika, a sweeper, was living very near and he was seen sweeping the stretch between Panchavati and Panchamundi altar daily with particular care and attention. It was observed by a devotee daily, which raised a question in his mind: "Rasika sweeps that portion daily very carefully; why?" One morning when Rasika was on the job, he was asked the reason. Rasika wanted not to reply, but the gentleman-devotee insisted on a specific answer. Seeing that he could not avoid the devotee Rasika told the reason with a request that the same should not be made public as long as he lived. As such, the incident given below, was made public only after the departure from this world of Rasika.

It was a summer black fortnight and the visibility was very poor at night. The heat was unbearable that night and Rasika came out in the open since he was not getting sleep. He started walking towards the temple aimlessly. At that time Thakur Shri Ramakrishna was very much present there. Suddenly Rasika saw that deep darkness prevailed everywhere but the area where the Panchamundi altar stands was illuminated. Rasika specifically wanted to know the reason why the place was illuminated in that darkness. When he approached the place he found that Thakur was sitting on the altar and the area was bright with the light emitted from his body only. Seeing the luminous body of Thakur Rasika lost consciousness and collapsed on the ground.

When Rasika regained consciousness after some time he saw that he was lying on the ground with his head on the lap of Thakur who was sprinkling water on his face. Thakur Ramakrishna was the priest of the temple and Rasika being only a sweeper the uncomfortable feeling in Rasika can be easily understood. Rasika asked: "Why am I here? Why did you touch me at this dead of night?"

Thakur replied: "Devotees of the Mother have no caste. But promise to me that whatever you have seen this night you will not disclose to anybody. Tell me what you want. Many devotees will come here in future. Keep the passage between Panchavati and Panchamundi clean. Sweep the same daily so that the Panchamundi altar is approachable to devotees."

Rasika replied: "Agreed. I shall keep the incident secret in my life time. But Thakur! You also promise to come on my departure day to take me along with you."

This incident was kept untold as long as Rasika lived. It is also understood that Thakur had kept the promise made by him to Rasika.

To this day Rasika is considered as one of the close devotees of Thakur Shri Ramakrishna Paramahamsa.

31

Choose a Time to Even Tell a Truth

LAPIDARIES HIRA and Moti had been close friends. In the precious stone trade both earned a good name. To avoid competition among themselves they decided to form a partnership with their mutual trust and personal expertise as capital. In course of time the firm made profits, and as appraisers of precious stones they became well known and were counted among the rich persons of the locality.

Moti had a small family. The house made by him had all amenities, and Moti, his wife Manimala and son Ratan were living happily. Wealth sometimes breeds vices. Suddenly, it was felt that more money was required to run the household. Manimala discovered that her husband Moti had taken to gambling. Slowly the family ran into debts. When debts mounted Moti did not know what to do. He could not leave his gambling habit either, and one day he committed suicide leaving his family in doom and gloom.

The death of Moti had put Manimala in dire straits. Ratan was still in school. The creditors who had lent money to Moti began pestering Manimala. In this hopeless situation she asked Hira for advice as to how to fend off the creditors and to run the household in the absence of any income. Hira said, "Bhabhiji! Moti was just like my elder brother. Just think in this way. Ratan will complete his graduation in three years from now. But if I make Ratan an expert appraiser of precious stones in these three years how good it will be! If you can send Ratan to the shop from tomorrow the training can start immediately." Manimala and Ratan both agreed to the proposal. The partnership business was revived, and Moti's family was getting regular income once again.

When the monetary condition improved, the old creditors started haunting again for the balance money. Suddenly Manimala remembered that her husband had given her three precious stones telling her: "Keep these stones. At the right time the same shall be useful." She took out the stones and through Ratan sent the same to Hira with a message: "If these are sold now, the creditors can be paid, and there won't be any debts." Hira took the stones and after examining those returned the same to Manimala with the message, "Bhabhiji, I will personally come and discuss the matter with you in the evening." Hira met Manimala and told her, "Bhabhiji! Ratan is steadily improving and becoming an expert. Let me give the money for the time being to clear off the debts. You can pay me back in easy instalments and whenever convenient. Market is not favourable now for selling these gems. At the right time, I will take necessary action. Don't worry."

Slowly three years passed. Ratan was well established in place of Moti now. He had become an expert appraiser of precious stones. The good days returned to Manimala's family. They had also paid back to Hira the money he advanced. One day Hira said to Ratan: "Tell your mother that now the market has become favourable and the three stones she has can be sold out." The next morning Ratan came with the small box containing the stones and gave it to Hira. Hira said, "Ratan! You are an expert appraiser of precious stones now. Why don't you examine these yourself and fix up the market price." Ratan was happy with such a response from the uncle. He took out the stones one by one and after examining, threw them in the waste bin and said: "Uncle, these are not precious stones at all; simple coloured glass only. You must have known that already. Then, Why didn't you tell the same thing when I had brought those three years back?"

Hira replied: "Yes, I knew. To tell the truth there is always a right time. If I had told you three years back, neither you nor your mother would have believed me. If the faith in me was lost that day, you would not have become an expert appraiser. Our partnership firm also would have not run. Now you are a lapidary yourself. You will earn quite a lot. Don't you think that this is the right time to tell you the truth?"

Ratan was happy that today he had seen his father in the loving uncle.

32

Seeing the Lord is the Goal

AFTER RIGOROUS religious austerities the devotee got the rare opportunity to see Lord Shri Hari with his own eyes. The Lord said: "I am pleased with you. Ask for a boon." The devotee prostrated before Shri Hari repeatedly and said: "All my desires are fulfilled on getting an opportunity to see you. I do not want anything more than this." Even after repeated requests the devotee could not be made to agree to ask something. Then Shri Hari out of compassion on the devotee said: "All right. On my own, I am giving you something: The moment your shadow falls on somebody, he will get emancipated."

But the reaction of the devotee surprised the Lord. The devotee informed Shri Hari: "Lord! Now I feel the necessity of a boon from you." The Lord replied "Most surprising. A few minutes back you only said that you did not require anything! Suddenly what happened that you had to change your earlier decision within such a short time?" He replied: "With my shadow falling if somebody gets respite from the sin, disease and the three kinds of affliction (material, spiritual, and supernatural), I have no objection but you are to ensure that nobody comes to know that it has happened due to falling of my shadow on them. If they come to know they will make my life miserable. That will bring self-conceit within myself and I will be losing you for all time to come. As such kindly give me a boon that their reason for emancipation shall remain a top secret. Even that should not be known to me also."

Shri Hari smiled on hearing the answer. He said: "You come along with Me. I knew that you do not require a boon. I just wanted to test you."

33

Experience Divine Bliss in Raga Vasanta

MUGHAL EMPEROR Akbar was sitting on his Peacock Throne majestically. He had deep regards for people with special qualities and achievements and had selected nine such persons to honour his Council of Advisers — they are called "nine jewels" or *navaratnas*. The celebrated singer Tansen was one of the jewels. One day the Emperor asked Tansen to entertain everybody with his musical excellence. Tansen started showing his calibre with a song based on Raga Vasanta. The royal court heard the presentation and all those present including the Emperor were spellbound. When the presentation ended the royal court remained silent since nobody had the appropriate words to praise Tansen. At last Emperor Akbar himself broke the silence and said: "Just excellent! Tansen, you are no doubt a priceless gem. You will get everything you desire today. Let me know what you want."

Singer Tansen felt satisfied since he could please His Majesty. He replied: "That the Raga Vasanta presented by me could please you, is in itself a big reward. Beyond that I do not aspire for anything. But I feel that my knowledge of the *raga* is nowhere near to the expertise of my *guruji*. If you want to hear the real Raga Vasanta I would request Your Majesty to hear the same from my Guru Saint Haridasji residing in the dense forest in Vrindavana." Emperor Akbar issued an order to present Saint Haridas in the royal court and a messenger was immediately despatched to Vrindavana. Saint Haridas heard the royal command and replied: "I do not perform anywhere except in the Almighty's *durbara*. Going to the royal court is not possible for me. In case Emperor Akbar wants to hear the Raga Vasanta from me he should come to this cottage in the *durbara* of the Almighty."

With the reply from Saint Haridas Emperor Akbar got furious. He took that as impertinence against the Emperor. Emperor Akbar immediately ordered that the disobedient person be punished with a stroke of the sword and his head should be brought to the *durbara*. On hearing this decision the court-poet Tansen intervened and submitted: "Great Emperor Akbar! If you take the life of my Guruji Saint Haridas then who will sing for you Raga Vasanta?" Emperor Akbar realized his mistake in taking a hurried decision in rage. He was thankful to Tansen since he had saved him from committing a dreadful crime of killing a virtuous person without a genuine reason. He then sent a message to Saint Haridas that his proposal is accepted. To the messenger who carried this message Saint Haridas said: "The Emperor has to come alone, unarmed. He has to come as an ordinary person, even without shoes."

Emperor Akbar had enormous respect for talented people. He agreed to all conditions imposed by Saint Haridas. Dressed as an ordinary man, barefooted, he walked down to the cottage of the saint just to hear Raga Vasanta. He had left his army and royal attire at the outskirts of the dense forest.

The Emperor received a warm welcome from the saint. He was given a simple mat to sit on the ground. Before starting to sing, the saint said: "Emperor! when I sing most of the ferocious animals living in this dense forest assemble nearby and hear the song peacefully. They forget their malice and do not attack anybody. After completion of the song they return to their original places. Kindly do not be afraid of them since they will not harm you in any way." The Emperor agreed and Saint Haridas started showing his skill in presenting Raga Vasanta. The words of the saint came true and many wild animals came near the cottage to hear the music in the *durbara* of the Almighty. The excellence of the performance was beyond the imagination of the Emperor.

The unique presentation kept the Emperor silent for a long time even after the completion of the song. Akbar felt that he had experienced something extraordinary and divine on that day.

34

God Lives in all His Creations

ON THE OUTSKIRTS of the village there lived an ascetic of Sufi community. Persons knew him as Baba Farid. He was spending his time meditating on the Almighty. The people of the nearby villages used to visit the saint for his advices and blessings. He was open to all irrespective of caste, community or religion.

A Hindu woman used to live in the village. She had lost her husband and was living on the income she earned as a maid-servant in other's houses. The only aim she had was to bring up her only child. The small family always had scarcity and as such the life was full of hardships. One day the woman remembered that on the next day her son would enter the fifth year of his age. As such, for the welfare of her son, she decided to take him to Baba Farid for getting him blessed on his birthday.

She took leave from the workplaces on the birthday of her son. Her resources did not permit buying new clothes for her son. So she had kept ready a shirt duly washed for him to wear. The son was properly bathed and made ready with the previously washed shirt. She knew that Baba Farid likes *jalebi* (a kind of sweetmeat). So she bought some *jalebi*s with the five rupees saved by her with much difficulty and went to Baba Farid along with her son.

Baba Farid was very happy to see them. When he was told that that day was the fifth birthday of the boy, he embraced and blessed the boy and prayed to Allah for his welfare. Now the mother took out the *jalebi*s from the wicker basket and wanted Baba Farid to accept the same as their offering. Baba Farid told the mother that eating *jalebi*s during daytime was not possible since he was on fast because it was the month of Ramzan. The mother and son were disappointed and grieved that their offering was not accepted by the Baba. Shedding tears they left the place taking back the *jalebi*s. Seeing that his fast had made an indirect and adverse impact on the simple devotees the Baba also felt sorry and tears welled up in his eyes.

When the mother and child were about to leave the gate, the Baba called them back and said, "Don't feel bad, I will take the *jalebi*s if that pleases Allah." She asked: "But what about the mandatory fast undertaken by you to please Allah?" Baba replied: "But the Allah living within you seems to be weeping when I did not accept your offering. Let me first please that Allah now, and then think about Him who is not so near to me at this moment." While taking the *jalebi*s Baba Farid was looking at the happy face of the mother. He said: "I cannot forego the love of Allah residing within you."

35

Malice Only Brings Misery

A BRAHMANA after a prolonged period of penance was blessed with the rare opportunity to see the Supreme God Mahadeva in person. The brahmana wanted something from the Lord. Lord Shiva gave him a bell and blessed him: "You will get everything desired on ringing this bell, but whatever you get, your neighbour will get double the amount you get." The brahmana initially was very happy with the boon, but the malevolence deeply rooted within himself prevented him to ring the bell and fulfil his ambitions. He did not even tell his wife about the bell. He was, under no circumstances ready to tolerate the "double" prosperity of his neighbour. As such the bell gifted by Lord Mahadeva was lying unused in a remote corner of his house and poverty ruled over the brahmana's family with severity. At one time the poverty became so unendurable that the brahmana left his home, leaving his poor wife behind, in search of livelihood at a far off place. Expecting the return of the brahmana, his wife waited for months together.

A long time passed but there was no news of the brahmana. The poverty at home reached a peak and the wife of the brahmana was not able to tolerate it. She then decided to get some money by selling the old and unused things lying in the house. Of course, they included the Shiva's bell. When the lady of the house, thinking about the continued scarcity of food, removed the bell from the corner where it was lying, it rang once, and, what a surprise!, the whole house was filled with delicious food. Realizing that the bell has some mysterious power, she rang the bell repeatedly and asked for all other necessities, and then luxuries, of life. She got everything she wanted. When she came out of the house to tell her neighbour about what she got by the grace of the bell, she could not believe her eyes — her neighbour told her that by some luck she got so many things — more than her requirement — all of a sudden. For obvious reasons the brahmana lady did not disclose the secret of the bell to anyone.

Days and months passed, and one morning the brahmana returned home with some money. He saw a big building at the place where his humble house stood. When he saw a bigger building at his neighbour's plot, his initial happiness evaporated. He became extremely worried with the thought: "Did my wife ask for all this prosperity by ringing the bell?" His good wife told him all about the bell and her prosperity as well as about the prosperity of their neighbour. The brahmana was burning with jealousy and rage on learning about his neighbour's "double" prosperity because of his own bell. The malevolence had raised its hood again and made him restless insisting on counter action.

Unable to bear the prosperity of his neighbour he did a stupid thing. He rung the bell and asked: "Let me be blind of one eye, lame of one leg and let there be a big well below the foundation of my house. The boon was infalliable and the brahmana immediately became blind of one eye, lame of one leg and his residence partly got destroyed due to the well below the foundation. The neighbour, as per Lord Shiva's words, became totally blind and lame and a major portion of his house had sunk in the ground. The blind and lame neighbour ended his life due to the collapse of his residence and physical incapacity to move out.

The malevolence was smiling at the peculiar way the brahmana used it.

36

Who Has Paid Whose Debt?

THE FARMER was returning from the field one evening totally exhausted after a hard day's labour. On the way, he heard a distress cry from a teenager asking for help. He could not think of anything else but to run to the spot. On reaching the spot he learned that a boy while playing with a ball had got trapped in a marshy land and was gradually going deeper while trying to save himself. A large crowd had accumulated but they were discussing the incident and nobody looked serious in rescuing him. The farmer forgot about his tiredness and immediately engaged himself in the rescue act. He had a long piece of rope tied on his waist and he had also kept a wooden plank nearby. With these items the farmer fought the battle and was able to rescue the boy. The boy seemed to be from a rich family. The onlookers talked about the courage of the farmer and started praising him.

At that moment there landed the father of the boy. The rich father heard about the boldness of the farmer. He was extremely grateful to the farmer since he had saved his son from near death. He wanted to reward the farmer but the farmer replied: "It was my moral duty to save the child and I have performed that only. I do not think that it calls for a reward." Repeated requests from the rich man could not make the farmer agree to accept some money.

On the scene appeared another young boy, the son of the farmer, who had come in search of his father since his usual time of return from work was long over. The rich man enquired about this boy and learned that although the boy was a meritorious student in the school, he had to discontinue studies due to paucity of funds. Now a proposal came from the rich man: "If I take charge of the monetary part of the education of your son, I hope, you will not have any objection." To this the farmer could not say "no."

Time cycle rolled on. The son of the farmer ascended the steps of knowledge with more and more honours with the monetary support from the rich man and at a certain point established himself as a great scientist and known to the world for his research and discovery of the wonder medicine penicillin.

The son of the rich man had also risen to be a great statesman in his country. Illness does not spare any one, even the prime minister of the country who was none other than our rich man's son. The wonder medicine discovered by the farmer's son finally saved the life of this great politician.

The farmer's son was Alexander Fleming and the richman's son was Sir Winston Churchill. Now the question remains unsolved: "Who has repaid whose debt?"

37

The Human Body is a Mosque

THE SAUNTERING ascetic was enjoying the company of heavenly bliss. He was brought back to this mundane world by a roar of thunder. He looked up at the sky and saw that it was jammed up with dark clouds. Gale with heavy shower looked an imminent danger, and so he started walking fast.

The nearest habitation was a city surrounded by a boundary wall having a main gate to enter. Rahim, the ascetic, tried his best to reach the Liongate before being hit by the downpour but although he beat the start of the rain, he could not reach the entry gate before it was closed. Hence, Rahim had to accept his night-stay outside the city facing unfavourable weather conditions. He knew that entry into the city was not possible before the next morning. At this time, he saw a dilapidated mosque-like building at a distance. He ran to the building to take shelter from the rain. The ascetic tried to push open the main door but the small push, however, was enough to cause the mosque-like structure to collapse. Rahim took the same as Allah's desire and decided to spend the night under a tree. That night it had rained heavily and the *fakir* Rahim enjoyed the beauty of nature while it was raining, and again dived into the sea of divinity.

The rains had stopped and the hour for opening of the Liongate arrived. The local people saw a *fakir* walking inside the city and were extremely thankful to Allah for the company of the divine person at the start of the day. The *fakir* was given a warm welcome by the residents who provided all the services he required. Sitting comfortably with the devout persons he narrated his previous night's experiences including the collapse of the abandoned mosque. Many people heard him, but some miscreants twisted and blew up the mosque episode and spread the word that the *fakir* demolished the holy mosque. The story got exaggerated and was presented to the Badshah also. The Badshah was furious and deputed his police to arrest the *fakir* and put him for trial.

At the court Rahim was told that since he had committed a heinous crime of demolishing a mosque he was being charged for the same. The *fakir* tried to convince the court that it was only accidental and not at all intentional. But in the court nobody listened to his reasonings and he was awarded capital punishment, i.e. death by hanging. The *fakir* was taken to the place of execution.

Even at this hour of distress the *fakir* maintained his cheerful countenance. Before execution, as per the normal practice, Rahim was asked about his last wishes. The *fakir* said, "Remove the shackles from my hands and I want the Badshah to witness my execution." After his last wishes were fulfilled, the *fakir* raised both his hands upwards and said, "Badshah! You ordered my execution for being an indirect and accidental cause for the collapse of a dilapidated and unused mosque. Here is a living mosque, my head is the dome, my hands are the minarets, and Allah is within me. You are about to demolish this living mosque. For this crime what punishment should you get?" The Badshah understood his folly, released the *fakir,* and sought his pardon.

38

Work and Earn

IN AN ISOLATED village in Rajasthan the rich man was on the verge of leaving this mortal world. The person was very old, was totally bedridden and was surrounded by his three sons. The sons were definitely worried about the imminent departure of their beloved father but were more anxious about what property they would inherit after his death.

The father could foresee the reason for his sons' worry. He asked somebody to call the head of the panchayat and two eminent persons of the village. This job was done with lightning speed. The sick father smiled at the alacrity of his sons in this case. In the presence of everybody the father announced the division of his property to ensure that the same is faithfully done after his departure. He said: "Half of my property will be inherited by the eldest son, followed by one third by the second son and one-ninth by the third son." At last the father announced that he has seventeen camels only as his property.

The next scene was completely different from the previous one. The crowd around the sick bed had disappeared; all had assumed that he was no more. Now, the property left by him seemed more important. In that state of extreme illness, he could clearly hear the discussions between his sons in the adjacent room. Some of the words and comments were most interesting — here are a few samples: "Property amassing without thinking about future disbursement," "Person without basic wisdom," "How to divide seventeen," "Does not have ability to do anything properly!," "Does not deserve so much firewood during cremation," "Even two bamboos are not required, only one will do to have him tied up to the same." The sick old man remembered the words of his *guruji*: "Know who is your near and dear. Except God, nobody." The father wanted to inform the sons: "Even now with a little help I can walk down to the cremation ground to save a lot of money for you."

Neither the sons nor the panchayat members knew how to divide seventeen camels by half, one-third or one-ninth. When they were in a fix they saw an outsider passing that way on a camel's back. When approached by the sons, the outsider understood the problem and said, "I find that the solution to this problem is very easy. The actual owner of the property in my eyes is a very intelligent person." The sons were not interested in the praise of their father's wisdom and only wanted to know the solution. The outsider said, "Suppose I give my camel to you on loan for some time. That will make 18 camels as your property. 18 can easily be divided by half, by 3 and by 9 totalling 17 camels and leaving my camel extra. One thing is sure, I won't give my camel on loan because I want to reach my place quickly. So the only solution is that all the three of you sons should work hard, buy a camel and add it to your father's property so that it can be divided as your father wanted. Instead of only enjoying inherited property, acquire more property through hard work."

39

Devotional Music Takes You to the Lord

RAMANANDA ROY was the minister to King Prataparudra. Ramananda, being honest and sincere, had earned a lot of respect from the king who used to consult him in his family matters also. The minister being totally dispassionate and least bothered about worldly pleasures, kept a distance from the king's royal life.

One day the devout Ramananda learned that Shri Chaitanya Mahaprabhu had come to a place which is very near to the estate. He immediately informed the king, who asked his minister to visit the holy man and pay respects. Ramananda was more than happy with his *darshana* of the Mahaprabhu, and wanted his king also to meet him. The Mahaprabhu said he had nothing to do with king and declined to see Prataparudra, but would certainly be glad to meet the king's little son who is a devotee of Lord Shri Krishna.

While sending his son to have an audience with Shri Chaitanya the king asked his minister Ramananda Roy to find out from the holy man the best way to meet him.

After the Mahaprabhu met the young prince, he did not like wounding the king's feelings and whispered in the ear of the minister the way by which the monarch can come to him.

Ramananda brought his master Prataparudra near the Mahaprabhu when he was in a state of *samadhi*. As suggested, King Prataparudra dressed as an ordinary man and barefooted, started reciting the verse *tava kathamritam* . . . from *Gopi Gita* of *Shrimad Bhagavata* with complete devotion. Hearing the sweet melody the *samadhi* of the Mahaprabhu was broken, and he called Prataparudra near and embraced him lovingly — the king now understood what divine bliss was. At that moment Prataparudra became a great devotee and vowed to spread the message of Lord Shri Chaitanya Mahaprabhu in his kingdom.

40

Surrender Totally to God

A WISE MONK was answering questions put up by devotees in a holy gathering. Somebody wanted to know: "We hear that the Lord appears Himself when His devotee is in distress. Can some example be given to substantiate the statement?" The monk narrated the following in reply.

Everybody knows that the Lord appeared from the pillar when his devotee Prahlada was in distress. This was a case of the Lord's direct intervention. Now a story of indirect intervention is presented.

Two birds were sitting on the branch of a tree hidden by the leaves. They were watching the falcon hovering above in the sky. The birds face imminent danger if they fall in the sight of the falcon above and hence they were waiting for the killer falcon to fly out. But they were dumbstruck to see a fowler on the ground lifting his bow and aiming his arrow at them. Now the birds were in a dilemma. If they keep sitting on the branch they would be killed by the fowler and if they fly out the falcon would get them. They resigned to their fate and wanted to see how the Almighty saves them. It was a total surrender before god. The Lord could not sit idle in such a situation. He had to save the birds directly or indirectly. He opted for the second path. Before despatch of the arrow a poisonous snake bit the fowler and he died instantaneously. The birds saw that god had saved them.

One day Lord Narayana was sitting for his meal. The food had been served. Suddenly he left the place in a hurry and returned to his seat within a moment. Lakshmi, the divine consort of Narayana, asked him about His momentary disappearance. The Lord replied: "I saw somebody had lifted a stick to hit my dear devotee and rushed to the spot to help him. But when I saw that the devotee had also lifted a stone to protect himself, I came back."

41

Divinity Sees no Sin in Man

It was one of the auspicious Saturdays when the pious Paramahamsadeva of Dakshineswara was scheduled to visit one of his dear devotees, Dr. Rama Chandra Dutta, in his newly acquired garden house at Kankurgachi in the northern part of Kolkata. Girish was tossing restlessly between the walls of his theatre office, and the question before him was whether to go or not. Girish as a playwright, poet, composer and actor, was a very respected person of that time. But his arrogance along with addiction to wine and women made this genius not acceptable to the so-called creamy layer of the society. Girish knew that the host of the day was very little known to him and he was sceptical about the type of welcome he would be extended in that house. But the attraction to go near the divine personality was also very powerful, and Girish himself did not know how he had landed near Dutta's house.

Rama Chandra Dutta's house was decorated tastefully and the host and his friend Surendra were at the door to welcome the vast number of people invited that day. His Holiness arrived ahead of Girish and with all respect he was guided to the venue of celebration. The celebration started and the devotees present started getting drenched in the shower of divinity. The holy man from Dakshineswara was in the centre of celebration shining like the crest jewel.

Girish's apprehension was proved wrong when he reached the venue. He was welcomed by the host and Surendra at the entrance and was led into the house by the host himself. Girish had met His Holiness only once earlier, but when he was seen coming near, the Paramahamsa recognized him at once. Girish fell at the feet of the holy man and begged for grace from him. The master gave him the touch of his palm and blessed him. There was a sudden change within Girish. The dramatist had a dramatic transformation. The feeling that he was a sinner had gone and in him grew a faith that he was now a blessed soul.

When the celebrations came to an end, everybody was served dinner. Some people, however, objected to everybody dining together raising a caste barrier. The objection was overruled saying that devotees do not have any caste or creed, and all of them took food together. The word "devotee" got a special status from that day onwards.

Paramahamsadeva, after dinner, came back to the central hall again and was immediately surrounded by devotees. Girish had already surrendered to the holy man and was considering him as his *guru*. Now he got a chance to ask some questions privately. He asked: "Shall the crookedness go?" Even after getting the answer in the affirmative, he wanted to hear the same thrice. The other devotees intervened and said: "When he has said

"Yes" then why ask again and again." The Master saw in the eyes of Girish the faith which he had not seen in anybody else. Girish was calm and contented.

On daybreak the devotees started assembling near the pious man at Dakshineswara. They all wanted to hear something from Him. The subject discussed on that morning was the development of faith in Girish. The amount and strength of faith was given a new name "twenty *annas*" (i.e. hundred and twenty-five per cent)*. At this time Girish also joined them. He was now intoxicated again, but with a change — god-intoxicated instead of wine-intoxicated.

---

* A rupee had sixteen *annas*.

42

Pray for Liberation

THE PRISON had been awarded "reformatory" status long back. That day the President was scheduled to visit the centre to check personally the conditions prevailing in the jail. Every official of the reformatory was extremely busy in giving finishing touches to the arragements. The prisoners were given proper instructions in regard to the etiquettes and manners to be followed in the presence of the President and during the scheduled question-answer session. On arrival at the jail the president called the jailor along with other officials and informed them that he will be visiting all the cells one by one and he wants to hear the answers to his questions from the prisoners only and that jail officials are not supposed to speak out unless asked. This instruction was not, however, liked by the jail officials but they had to obey the President.

To everybody's surprise the president started his inspection from the cells only. The programme chalked out by the officials was sidetracked and it looked like the President was not at all interested in the normal welcome function, or the kitchen, or anything else.

The President entered the first cell, and as planned the prisoner in a brand new jail uniform got up and bowed to His Excellency. The President then asked the prisoner, "Do You have any complaint about anything?" The prisoner replied: "Your Excellency! I am very comfortable here but the walls of the cell have not been whitewashed for long. If the same can be arranged, I shall be most grateful." The President instructed the jailor accompanying him to get the same done at the earliest.

After this the President walked down to the cells one by one and the prisoners asked for some additional facilities (viz. another blanket, two additional breads, improvement in quality of vegetable served in the meals, etc.). Before the President, the jailor and other officials promised to redress all the prisoners' grievances. The prisoners were very satisfied with the patient hearing given to them by the head of the land.

Now only one cell was left out, and the president entered the cell and put the same question to that prisoner also. The prisoner answered politely: "Your Excellency, You are gracious and I hold great respect for you. I pray to you that I should be released from the prison. I am here for a very long time, and frankly speaking I do not even remember why and for what crime I am kept here. Kindly grant me freedom." Everybody present was surprised when they heard the President telling: "Agreed, he is to be released immediately."

Common people while praying to god ask for wealth, prosperity, promotion and items giving worldly pleasures, instead of freedom or emancipation from this world of births and deaths.

43

Bitter Medicine Helps

IT WAS a seminary giving expertise in music. One morning the guru of the institution told a certain student that he will be taking his final examination in the presence of all the other students. The practice of classical music was going on for a long time, and the student hoped that after passing the test he could become a qualified musician.

At the scheduled time the student sat with the *tanapura* to display his ability. The *guru* asked the student to show his expertise in Raga Bhupali. The student liked the particular *raga* and presented it to the audience, with all sincerity and knowledge at his command. The *ashrama* residents heard the *raga* and were spellbound with the display. When the performance ended the *guru* appreciated the presentation, but everybody present was surprised when they heard that the *guru* wanted to hear the Raga Bhupali once again from the student.

Superclass presentation followed. The *guru* praised the student's expertise once again but asked him to repeat the same once more. People around could not follow why the venerable *guru* was asking the student to present the same *raga* again. The *guru* went on asking the student to sing Raga Bhupali and the student had to sing the same again and again. When the student got the *guru*'s instruction for the fifteenth time he submitted: "Guruji! If you permit, may I sing in some other *raga*?" The *guru* replied: "Unless you present Raga Bhupali correctly, I am not going to spare you. There is no mistake in the *raga* display. The mistake is in its presentation."

The student wanted to know the fault so that the same could be rectified. The *guru* told the student: "A few years back when I had started imparting the science of music I had told you that this human body is the instrument *vina*. While the head and the body are the two extreme parts of *vina*, the neck is the connecting part which produces melody. If the strings are fixed too tight or too loose the *vina* will not be able to produce the correct sound. Your Bhupali is excellent but you are presenting the *raga* keeping your body tight. Your body *vina* is not in the desired condition. Unless you are relaxed and keep your body in a relaxed condition the display and presentation of music will not be able to impart divinity in the form of pleasure and bliss to the listeners. So my son, shed off anxiety and with full faith on your own ability present the Raga Bhupali to all of us. If you do so you will also get the share of bliss along with the listeners."

The student came down to get the blessings of his *guru*. He now saw a supreme *vaidya* in his *guru* who gives bitter medicine to the patient forcibly if necessary. He considered himself very fortunate to have been trained by him.

44

Patronize the Worthy

THE ASCETIC lived in his *ashrama* a little away from the hullabaloo of the busy township. He was alone in his *ashrama* spending time in meditation on the Lord of the Universe. People from distant places were visiting the ascetic in search of peace of mind. They all got advice in spiritual matters. Nobody used to go back without full satisfaction.

One day somebody dropped in at the *ashrama*. The person wanted permission from the ascetic to stay in the *ashrama* to serve him. The ascetic said that any particular requirement for services did not exist with him at that time since he was capable to do all the work himself. But the newcomer told him that he wanted to stay there as a cook. The permission was finally granted. While the ascetic was totally immersed in meditation and reading of scriptures, the newcomer started cooking food in the *ashrama*. The so-called new cook seemed to be well versed in music and while cooking he was always heard singing in a low voice.

That day the *ashrama* was visited by a rich person. While enjoying the company of the ascetic, he could hear the classical music sung by the cook in the kitchen area. He made a request to the venerable ascetic, "Your cook has a flair and knowledge in music. Kindly permit me to arrange for his proper training in music at my cost." The ascetic gave permission at once and the cook was taken out of the *ashrama* that day by the rich man to some classical music preceptor. From that day onwards the cook started getting trained in classical music, but he continued with the cooking service to the ascetic also. Three years passed, and the cook earned a certificate in classical music and he became a person of repute among the public. He got a national award as well. Being an established music performer he became a respected person and started going up in the ladder of popularity. In this process his association with the *ashrama* broke down.

A long time elapsed. Attaining to a top position, the new music exponent remembered the grace of the ascetic in the *ashrama*. The meditative peaceful atmosphere of the *ashrama* was calling him continuously. The expert did not have the strength to brush aside the call of the *ashrama* atmosphere and one day he again landed at the *ashrama*. The ascetic was very pleased to see him after a long time. After normal inquiries about the well-being, the expert was surprised to know that the revered ascetic kept all updated information about him. Suddenly, he asked the ascetic permission to stay in the *ashrama* for a few days. When he was asked: "What do you want to do here now," the answer came: "Cooking." As such in the spiritual meditative atmosphere the old cook was reinstated. Along with the cooking the singing at low voice went on.

One day the rich person again visited the *ashrama*. He heard the music at low voice. He asked the ascetic: "Such an expert in classical music is cooking in your *ashrama*?" The ascetic replied: "Earlier the cook used to sing at a low voice and now the expert in music is cooking. Where is the difference? I am calling him. Please put this question to him only." The musician was asked the same question. He replied: "I have come to visit my mother. This *ashrama* only gave birth to my music and nurtured it. Unless the atmosphere is created, good music can never flourish." The rich man was very happy with the answer since his decision in identifying the special quality in a person got certified that day.

45

Brahman is Immortal

THE RAJARSHI or royal-ascetic Janaka was enjoying the association of saints and ascetics who had assembled at Mithila to meet him. The learned guests were given accommodation in the royal palace only. That day the guests were talking on spiritual matters, particularly on the knowledge of *Brahman*. The king listened to everybody but did not give any opinion or comments. The guests saw that Janaka was not commenting on their views and was keeping mum. After repeated requests from the visiting saints and ascetics the *brahmagyani* Janaka said: "The true knower of *Brahman* should remain contented with the dispensation of providence." This simple reply did not satisfy the persons who were trying to advertise their deep knowledge about *Brahman*. King Janaka smiled at their reactions.

Suddenly there was a great chaos in the far remote corner. When the cause of the disturbance was enquired into, it became known that there was a fire raging in the royal palace. The persons who were discussing deep philosophy in regard to *Brahman* a few minutes back got up from their seats and started running towards the burning portion of the royal palace. Only the royal ascetic Janaka remained on his seat. He seemed to be least bothered about the incident. He was, however, amused at the reactions of the visiting saints and ascetics.

After some time one of the saints came back to the company of Janaka. The king asked the saint: "Saint! why did you go that fast on hearing the incident of fire in the royal palace?" The saint replied: "In the open my inner garment was getting dried up near that particular part of the royal palace which was under fire. I wanted to remove and save the loincloth before it got burnt out!" The royal ascetic Janaka, on hearing the same, laughed heartily. He murmured: "Is that your knowledge of *Brahman*!"

The saint was surprised with the reaction of the king. He asked the Mithila monarch: "There was a fire reported in your own palace but there was not any anxiety seen in you! It looked that you were least bothered about the fire."

Janaka started laughing heartily again and said, "*Brahman* is spread everywhere in this world. *Brahman* is eternal and immortal. Can the fire burn out *Brahman*? What is your opinion?"

The saint understood that the knowledge of *Brahman* is known to the royal ascetic in its true perspective. The real knower of *Brahman* has seen *Brahman* even in the fire.

46

Have Firm Faith in God

THE POET GHALIB was termed as love personified since his creations are soaked in the sap of love. The persons who are well fascinated by the writings of Ghalib know that his love is above the sense of human body and the same is totally submitted to the formless God — *Brahman* whom the religious people search for during their austere endeavours. Ghalib firmly believed that the all-powerful Allah does not live in a fixed place. He resides in the heart of the people who have been created by Him. To see Him you require spiritual vision and tears of love. For that the unclean heart mirror is washed first of all. For a spiritual vision one requires the grace of Allah and for the second part you require sustained perseverance. In the way of love it is easier to get Him. Hence, Ghalib used to distribute the sap of love in his writings.

Such a person also lived in a state of extreme poverty. his meals were uncertain on all days, but, for that, he had no complaint against anybody. The person who lives in close proximity of the Almighty cannot ask for insignificant items from the Lord. One of the great devotees of Ghalib used to tell him that Ghalib is facing the tyranny of poverty since he does not go to the mosque to pray to Allah. Once, he convinced Ghalib to go to the mosque and try. As such, to please the devotee Ghalib reached one of the mosques on a Friday.

Ghalib knew that before the prayer it was necessary to have a proper wash. As such, he also started doing the same before the prayer started along with others.

At this hour a very rich person saw the renowned Ghalib in the mosque. That person was also a firm devotee of Ghalib and actually held profound respect for the great man. He saw that Ghalib was having a wash to participate in the prayer session. He respected Ghalib as representative of the Almighty only. As such he asked: "Venerable Ghalib? You are here?" Ghalib told the devotee (who had also come to participate in the prayer session): "Somebody told me that if I pray then my poverty will go." The rich person wept to see the pitiable condition of the venerable person and said, "I can never imagine the poverty of a man of your repute." He gave a lot of wealth to Ghalib since he was sure that he is serving the Almighty standing incognito in front of him. Ghalib could see the grace of Allah in that rich person.

But the donor devotee saw a peculiar thing now. The respected Ghalib got up after the wash and started walking out of the mosque. The devotee ran after him. Ghalib told him: "If by wash only you are able to get the grace of Allah then why present a formal prayer?"

The devotee watched Ghalib with surprise. He appreciated the faith of the great man.

47

Purity Needs no Advertisement

IT WAS EARLY morning hour. The group of brahmanas were present on the shore of the Brahmabari river Ganga. The daily rituals were being performed to advertise their supremacy in the caste ladder — the long sectarian mark impressed with sandal paste on the foreheads (usually known as *tilaka*), wearing silk clothes, doing breathing exercises (usually known as *pranayama*). They were all wearing *namavali*, the piece of the scarf with the names of deities printed on it.

When the act was being played, there arrived an old brahmana who looked quite tired due to a long walk he had had covering a great distance. The condition of the feet of the newcomer was certifying the same. The brahmana kept his small bundle on the shore and got down in the Ganga to take bath. He completed his bath within a short time and changed his clothes quickly. After this he took out some flattened rice from his possession and started eating the same. The food was also eaten in a record short time and the brahmana drank three handfuls of Ganga water and was ready for walking back to his destination again.

The brahmanas present at the shore objected to such action and started criticising the new brahmana. They openly said: "What type of a brahmana are you? After taking bath you never bothered to undertake the essential rituals of the brahmana. You took food without doing any of the rituals which a normal brahmana is required to do daily. Even after this you want to be acknowledged as a caste brahmana ? You are not fit to be called brahmana from now onwards."

The visiting brahmana heard all the complaints calmly. Then he replied in clear words: "Possibly you all are not able to understand me properly. To obtain purity I have done everything. For a pure life a pure body is essential and I have achieved the same by taking a bath in Brahmabari Ganga and for internal purity I have had three handfuls of Ganga water. Now please tell me where I have erred."

The advertising brahmanas stood dumbfounded at the bank of river Ganga. They did not have any answer with them. The visiting brahmana had actually questioned them: "Is advertisement needed to show that you are a brahmana?"

48

Truth is Bitter

GAJANAN FACED a problem that day. Although he had a small family, poverty had been his constant companion. Over and above all this, a message received by him was troubling him. The message was to inform Gajanan that four guests would arrive at their residence the next day and would leave in the evening hours only. It was evident from the message that these people were required to be served with lunch. The family had acute shortage of cereals and vegetables. To get something from the grocer's shop was also not possible since the payment for the earlier purchases was still pending.

Gajanan discussed the matter with his wife. They believed that the guests before their departure would be giving at least ten rupees to their only son as a gift. The grocer was promised the payment by the evening and the food materials were collected from his shop on that condition.

The guests arrived as scheduled. They were served with excellent food and they were all pleased with the hospitality extended to them. They, however, did not bother to enquire what the host family took that day. They had a comfortable nap after the heavy lunch and at the scheduled hour prepared for departure. They also forgot to pay something to the small kid in the Gajanan family. But they remembered the same after going a little distance away. They called the small kid from a distance. After getting a little push from the mother, the boy agreed to go to the persons. The parent saw that the departing guests were trying to give something to the son but the boy was not agreeing to accept the same. The mother told the son by a gesture that whatever the guests are giving the boy he should accept it.

The boy now shouted back: "These people were supposed to give ten rupees but they are trying to give five rupees only."

The parents as well as the guests were all flabbergasted. The kid Narayana was telling the truth! Of Course, being a small child, he did not know that it was a bitter truth.